THE MAKING OF A MEXICAN AMERICAN MAYOR

THE MAKING OF A MEXICAN AMERICAN MAYOR

Raymond L. Telles of El Paso

By

MARIO T. GARCÍA

Professor of History and Chicano Studies

University of California, Santa Barbara

SOUTHWESTERN ✦ STUDIES NO. 105

© 1998
Texas Western Press
The University of Texas at El Paso
El Paso, Texas 79968-0633

First Edition
Library of Congress Catalog No. 97-060855
ISBN 0-87404-276-3

∞

Texas Western Press books are printed on acid-free paper, meeting the guidelines for permanence and durability of the Committee on Production Guidelines for Book Longevity of the Council on Library Resources.

*In Ambassador Raymond L. Telles's name
this book is dedicated to his wife, Delfina Telles,
and to his daughters,
Dr. Cynthia A. Telles and Dr. Patricia E. Telles.*

CONTENTS

ACKNOWLEDGMENTS

As in the writing of any study, many individuals and organizations share in its completion. I am first of all indebted to my campus, the University of California, Santa Barbara, for providing sabbatical leave as well as various research grants. I am particularly grateful to the National Research Council for a 1982–83 fellowship under which research for this project was conducted. A fellowship at the Woodrow Wilson International Center for Scholars in 1984 provided the stimulating and supportive environment for the first drafting of this manuscript.

In El Paso, I wish to pay thanks to Prof. Carl Jackson and my friends and fellow historians in the Department of History at the University of Texas at El Paso who so graciously hosted me during my research period. My *compañero* Prof. Oscar Martínez, then director of the Inter-American and Border Studies Program at UTEP, as in the past, provided me his friendship and support. Special thanks goes to Sarah John, then associate director of the Institute of Oral History at UTEP, who transcribed my lengthy interviews with Ambassador Telles and who supported the project by her friendship and numerous supplies of tapes for my oral interviews. César Caballero and Bud Newman at Special Collections in the UTEP Library likewise assisted me in research. Gilda Baeza and Mary Sarber at the El Paso Public Library as always provided professional assistance. Irma Silva at Southwest Micro-films proved to be an extra asset in my work. All of these friends and colleagues helped make El Paso feel like home again. I wish to thank Bill Reagen at the city clerk's office at El Paso City Hall for providing access to city council minutes. I am grateful to Nancy Hamilton for reviewing the manuscript and for suggesting updated revisions. Many thanks to Alexandro Valdez, the development alumni director at Cathedral High School in El Paso, for providing access to *The Chaparral*, the school yearbook that contained information on Raymond Telles. I owe gratitude to Rudy Gutiérrez at the *El Paso Times* for his assistance in obtaining copies of photographs used in the book, and to the *Times* and the *El Paso Herald-Post* for permission to reproduce particular photographs. I likewise wish to acknowledge the assistance of the staff at the *Times-Herald-Post* Library. At Texas Western Press, Marcia Daudistel strongly supported publication and Bobbi Gonzales lent her technical expertise. In addition, the anonymous reviewer of the manuscript provided important suggestions to strengthen it. Finally, I'm grateful to Darla McDavid for her careful typing and preparation of the manuscript.

Of course, I will be forever grateful to Ambassador Raymond L. Telles for the time he gave me as we probed his past and the trials and joys of the making of a Mexican American mayor. Yet, this story is not just the history of one man, but that of a whole community. The following persons welcomed me into their homes and offices and filled in the historical gaps of the Telles story: Lucy Acosta, Paul Andow, Judge Albert Armendáriz, Ted Bender, Dr. Raymond Gardea, Modesto Gómez, Francisco "Kiko" Hernández, Joe Herrera, Alfredo "Lelo" Jacques, E. B. Leon, Ray Marantz, Henry Martínez, Gabriel Navarrete, Alfonso Pérez, Conrad Ramírez, Belen Robles, Luciano Santoscoy, Ralph Seitsinger, Marvin Shady, Richard Telles, David Villa, and Delfina Telles.

Finally, I wish to thank my family in El Paso, especially Rosalva Montelongo, for providing familial attention as well as bread and board during various research trips there. And, as always, to Ellen and to my wonderful children, Giuliana and Carlo.

The Politics
of Status

T he election of Raymond L. Telles as mayor of El Paso in 1957 was a major breakthrough in the Mexican American quest for political representation and status in the United States. A personal triumph for Telles, his election also symbolized a political victory for the entire Mexican American community of this key southwestern border city. After over one hundred years of limited and inadequate political participation in local affairs, Mexican Americans concluded in 1957 that the time had come for electing one of their own as mayor of a city numbering almost 250,000 with one half of the population being of Mexican descent.[1] Telles became the first American of Mexican descent to be elected mayor of a major southwestern city in this century. His election and subsequent administration (1957–1961) stimulated additional Mexican American electoral initiatives and, more importantly, gave Mexican Americans a growing confidence in themselves as American citizens and as political actors. Hence, the Telles story is part of the larger and ongoing struggle by Mexican Americans to eliminate a legacy of second-class citizenship.

1

The role of Mexican Americans as second-class citizens origi-
nated with the conquest of northern Mexico by the United States
during the 1840s and in the subsequent labor exploitation of Mexicans in the Southwest. The annexation of this region assumed
major economic significance by its integration as a supplier of key
industrial raw materials (copper, lead, and silver) as well as agri-
cultural and cattle foodstuffs to feed the industrial armies of the
East and Midwest. The railroads penetrated the Southwest and
northern Mexico, opening these areas to American capital and
technology. In turn, southwestern entrepreneurs induced Mexicans to cross the border and work as cheap unskilled labor. Consequently, social relations in the Southwest and in communities such
as El Paso took on definite economic characteristics. Mexicans, for
the most part, served as manual laborers while Anglos possessed
highly skilled jobs as well as managerial, business, and professional
occupations. Mexican workers in this exploitative relationship produced much wealth, but received little of it in return.[2]

The labor exploitation of Mexicans supported by racial and cultural discrimination likewise led to their political second-class status. A small number of acculturated and better-off Mexican Americans did participate in early El Paso politics, but as political ward
bosses for the Democratic "Ring" that controlled local politics during the nineteenth and early twentieth centuries. Most Mexicans
possessed no real political representation. Many, of course, prior to
the 1930s maintained Mexican citizenship. Still, they contributed to
El Paso politics by being paid to vote by unscrupulous Anglo politicians acting through Mexican American intermediaries. Mexicans
received slight patronage as city laborers out of this political
arrangement, but on the whole their involvement only supported a
political system that reinforced their economic oppression. Mexican
immigrant workers undergoing a process of proletarianization
struggled to protect themselves, but their vulnerable political status
as "aliens" and their personal desires to return to Mexico did not
lend themselves to long-lasting protest movements.[3]

World War II, however, proved to be a political watershed for
Mexican Americans. A new generation—the Mexican American

generation—came of age that unalterably refused to accept second-class status and that was prepared to wage protracted struggles for their civil rights. Not immigrants like most of their parents, these mostly first-generation U.S.-born Mexicans achieved
slightly improved working-class positions for themselves as a
result of greater needs for better-trained workers in a more com-
plex southwestern economy plus increased access to public education. In the process, some began to perceive themselves as an
exploited social class. Moreover, a distinct Mexican American
lower middle class composed of small businessmen and smaller
numbers of professionals also evolved and began to become aware
of its own class interest. Changing class characteristics accompanying American economic revival in turn produced growing political
and social expectations and aspirations among many younger
Mexican Americans. Socialized to American democratic principles
through the schools and mass media and patriotically serving in
World War II, these Mexican Americans sought to eliminate barriers to full equality with other citizens.[4]

Repulsed by overt forms of social discrimination, Mexican
Americans after the war chose to first confront segregation in public facilities such as schools, theaters, swimming pools, restaurants,
housing tracts, and access to elective offices. The efforts to force
respect for Mexican Americans by pursuing an integrationist strategy involved what Ladd in his study of black politics in the South
terms "status goals" as opposed to "welfare goals" intended to
obtain material improvements without disturbing race-ethnic divisions.[5] For Mexican Americans, as for many blacks after the war,
"status goals" meant abolishing those forms of public discrimination that called attention to their race and ethnic difference. Con-
sumed by a desire to be treated as full-fledged American citizens,
Mexican Americans engaged in the "politics of status." "The
demand for integration . . . ," Ladd notes, "is essentially the attempt
by a group which has been branded inferior in quite literally a
thousand ways by white Americans to gain recognition as a truly
equal partner in the American democracy."[6] Reformist by nature,
the "politics of status" did not directly combat the root cause of

Mexican American underdevelopment in the Southwest: the need by capital to expand from maintaining most Mexicans as pools of cheap and surplus labor. The altering of this relationship would entail more fundamental struggles, encompassing both sides of the border, than most Mexican American leaders in the postwar era were both ideologically and politically prepared to undertake. They believed that the system was capable of reforming inequities. Nevertheless, the "politics of status," including the struggle for democratic political rights, marked a forward step in the political evolution of Mexican Americans. The rising expectations generated by this movement, as well as its accompanying frustrations, would result in even more challenging efforts by a succeeding generation.

In El Paso, Mexican Americans interpreted status goals predominantly in electoral political terms. Unlike other parts of Texas where Mexicans faced de facto racial discrimination in public facilities, Mexican Americans in the border city did not; they had historically possessed access—if they could afford it—to theaters, restaurants, stores, and other forms of public facilities. Even schools and housing tracts were not strictly segregated in El Paso. The Anglo power structure had early learned that it made little economic sense to exclude Mexicans from public facilities due to their importance as a source of labor and as consumers.[7] Moreover, discrimination against Mexicans would jeopardize El Paso's relation with Mexico, especially the border city's role as a labor center and as a wholesale and retail outlet for northern Mexican customers. Not confronting a system of overt public discrimination, Mexican Americans, however, still lagged behind Anglos in jobs, wages, education, and political representation.[8] "El Paso's discrimination," one report on El Paso politics concluded, "is based primarily on the belief, or rationale, that Latins are 'not qualified' (primarily because of lack of education) for various jobs."[9] In 1950, for example, the Spanish-surnamed population in El Paso composed more than half of the city's total population. Of these, almost three-quarters of Mexican Americans were born in the United States. Despite their numbers, Mexican Americans constituted only 1.8 percent of high white-collar occupations, only 26.4 percent of low white-collar occupations, and only 11.2 percent of skilled blue-collar ones. Only seven Mexican American lawyers practiced in El Paso.[10] Hence, by mid-century Mexican Americans still formed, despite certain gains, a predominantly working-class population excluded from access to political and economic power. Two El Pasos continued to coexist as they had since the nineteenth century: one more affluent and mostly Anglo in the northern section of the city and the other relatively poor and mostly Mexican "south of the tracks." As two scholars described this physical duality:

> The ecology of the city reflects the local ethnic situation. Stretching along the Rio Grande River, the city is split into two spurs by the insistence of Mt. Franklin close to the city center. . . . Highway 80 is roughly a north-south axis. Below this highway the population is made up primarily of recent Mexican arrivals. They are mostly unskilled and semi-skilled workers and represent the poorest segment of the community. . . .
>
> As one moves north of Highway 80 up the spurs to the higher territory, the proportion of Mexican and Spanish-name residents decreases. There is no strict residential ethnic segregation in El Paso, as is commonly found in other Texas cities. In general, Spanish-name persons reside in areas commensurate with their social and economic status. Since few of them are in the upper middle or upper classes, residential areas of this level are populated primarily by Anglos.[11]

In 1948, writer-historian Carey McWilliams visited the city and wrote "The El Paso Story" in *The Nation*:

> That progressive political action is badly needed in El Paso was apparent at once. Many of the poorer Mexican families live in old adobe houses built around an interior court in which is a central hydrant for water. A recent survey of the housing conditions of 200 families (7.06 persons per family) living in such courts revealed 10.06 families using a single toilet (71.02 persons per toilet!) and showed that only 5.05 percent of the dwellings had shower facilities, only 3 percent bathtubs, and only 3 percent private toilets. For many years the great majority of the deaths among children from

typhoid fever, smallpox, scarlet fever, whooping cough, measles, diphtheria, enteritis, and diarrhea have been reported from South El Paso, where most of the Mexicans live. Although an increasing number of Spanish-speaking students are finishing high school and going to college, these young people find the range of occupations open to them so limited that they seldom stay in El Paso. A leading merchant told me that one of his truck drivers, of a Spanish-speaking family, enlisted in the army at the outbreak of war and rose to the rank of captain. On leaving the service this man tried to find some employment offering better opportunities, but after a few months he applied for his old position.[12]

Under such circumstances, Mexican Americans in El Paso—experiencing both poverty and degrees of progress—viewed the attainment of effective political representations as the first step in equalizing their status with Anglos. Not having to struggle, as in other parts of Texas, for the right to integrate public facilities—already achieved in El Paso—Americans of Mexican descent in the border city instead saw their lack of access to electoral offices as the most significant affront to their status as American citizens. No one from this ethnic group had ever been elected mayor nor served on the city council between 1900 and 1950.[13] Moreover, the existence of a poll tax in Texas added to the political disenfranchisement of many Mexican Americans. After the war, leaders from this community vowed to change this. "The Spanish-speaking group is ripe for organized action and has an endless list of social grievances, many of which date back fifty years," McWilliams wrote of El Paso. "It has only begun to achieve real political maturity, but leaders are emerging and the day of political reckoning cannot be long deferred."[14] This was especially true for the aspiring lower middle class that considered politics not only as an avenue of personal mobility, but more importantly of collective respectability. These Mexican Americans believed that the most symbolic way of acquiring status as full-fledged American citizens was through electoral success including winning the mayor's office. It is in this context that the political ascendance of Raymond Telles can be appreciated.

CHAPTER ONE

The Young Raymond Telles

If the election of Raymond Telles in 1957 as mayor of El Paso had wider implications, his personal success can be better understood by the type of family socialization he experienced. Telles proved to be the most "electable" Mexican American candidate in El Paso from no mere stroke of luck. It involved his more fortunate family circumstances.

The Telles family stressed four particular qualities: a disciplined personality and character; an emphasis on education and personal improvement; compassion for people, especially the downtrodden; and concern for the political and civic improvement of the Mexican American community. Each of these influences would serve Raymond Telles well in his personal life and in his public career.

Discipline and hard work formed the foundation of the Telles family. Ramón Telles, Raymond's father, did not avoid challenges. He came from an old established family going back to the late

Telles family home, 918 South St. Vrain, 1940.
Courtesy Raymond L. Telles

eighteenth century in Ysleta, downriver from El Paso. Rather than remaining in the predominantly rural environment of Ysleta, where his father had inherited a Spanish land grant which he eventually lost, Ramón moved to El Paso where he became a hard-working bricklayer. He was an excellent bricklayer and was at times recruited to work in Albuquerque and Phoenix. Among his accomplishments was helping to construct St. Ignatius Catholic Church on Park Street in south El Paso.[1]

He married Angela López from Chihuahua in 1913. Utilizing his skill for his own benefit, he and his wife built a home of adobe and brick at 918 South St. Vrain close to the canal in El Segundo Barrio or the Second Ward, the major Mexican settlement in south El Paso and adjacent to the border. Although many recent Mexican immigrants lived in El Segundo Barrio, so also did many established families. Here, in her home, Angela Telles, with the aid of her mother as midwife, gave birth on 15 September 1915 to a son. They named him Ramón after his father and in memory of their first son who had died as an infant. Although named Ramón, the young Raymond Telles was called "Monchi" at home, a nickname for Ramón. Three other sons followed of whom two survived: José Ignacio and Ricardo.[2]

Life in south El Paso for the Telles children consisted of a strict upbringing. The parents strove to give their children a decent childhood and to instill in them a sense of ambition. Leery of their being corrupted by gangs that roamed the barrio, Ramón Telles prohibited his children from playing with unruly elements or straying too far from home. "[We] were forbidden to join any of these gangs of kids," Raymond Telles recalls, "and if [Father] came home and we were across the street with some of these boys, why he would really give us a good whipping, and I mean a good one, with a horse whip." Richard Telles, Raymond's younger brother, notes that his father was a "mean hombre. He was a disciplinarian from the word 'go.'" Still, the Telles children played baseball in the streets and roller-skated, although always careful to be back at home when their father returned from work. They also used the nearby Franklin Canal as a swimming pool despite its dangerous currents. Of the two older brothers, José, or "Nacho" as he was called, proved to be the one who most often incurred the wrath of his father, while Raymond, according to Richard, as a child was more passive. Raymond Telles recalls that if his father came home and found them across the street, he and his two brothers would quickly run to Doña Estefana's house, next door to the Telleses, where, in her kitchen where she was always making corn tortillas, the little old lady would protect them from their father.[3]

To better prepare his boys for the toughness of south El Paso, their father taught them how to box. He, himself, was a good boxer and trained with professional boxers in a big open area near the Peyton Packing Company. The Telles boys often accompanied their father to the makeshift boxing ring. This training proved to be of use to Raymond, who apparently was not as passive as Richard

Angela Telles with children
(from left to right): Raymond, Richard, and José,
circa 1925.
Courtesy Raymond L. Telles

remembers him, in the barrio. "There was one big kid who always tried to beat up on us because we were smaller," Raymond recalls.

> I got tired of this and one day I told my brother Joe, "Let's you and I come up with a strategy to defend ourselves. When this guy comes up to me, I want you to have two hands full of dirt. When he approaches me, you throw the dirt in his eyes, then I'll go to work on him."

Brother Joe did as he was told, and Raymond proceeded to give the "tough" kid a boxing lesson.[4]

South El Paso proved hard, but Ramón Telles made life as comfortable as possible for his family. To relieve congestion and allow greater privacy, he expanded his home into one of the few

Don Ramón Telles and Richard Telles, circa 1930s. Courtesy Raymond L. Telles

two-story structures on the south side. Despite more space, all
three Telles boys slept in the same room. Moreover, Ramón Telles
did not have enough income to include private toilet facilities.
Instead, a common toilet and shower had to be shared with neighbors. Wood had to be gathered to be used as fuel to heat water for
cooking and baths. Flooding during the rainy season was also a
problem since the streets of south El Paso were unpaved.[5]

Religion in the form of Roman Catholicism formed a significant
part of family culture for the Telleses. Both parents were devout
Catholics and regular attendance at Sunday Mass was part of their
family ritual. In fact, it was a prerequisite for the boys to receive
their *domingo* or weekly allowance of five cents from their father.
Besides attending Mass at nearby St. Ignatius, every other Sunday
the Telleses would pile into their Ford Model T, which Telles's
father had converted into a sleek passenger vehicle that looked like a
racing car, and drive downriver to participate at Mass at one of the
missions, such as at Ysleta, Socorro, or San Elizario. At home,
Telles's mother prayed before an altar in honor of the Virgen de
Guadalupe. Moreover, Ramón Telles was a loyal member of the
Unión Católica San José, a mutual benefit society in the barrio dedicated to St. Joseph, that provided emergency assistance to its members as well as promoting Catholic culture in south El Paso.[6]

Discipline in the Telles home also involved an appreciation for
work. As a youngster, Raymond helped with family expenses by
shining shoes and selling newspapers in downtown El Paso. He
later washed cars for his father when Ramón Telles opened a
transfer and taxi stand on East Overland Street. In addition, he
helped to sell home-brewed beverages to his father's customers.
This included selling *horchata* made from cantaloupe seeds and
tesuino made from corn that was ground up and put into *jaros*
(jars). These drinks could be intoxicating. Later, while in high
school, Raymond assisted his mother in a small family grocery
store. "I was just a kid," Telles notes, "but I was supposed to be the
butcher. I didn't know anything about butchering . . . and I had to
try . . . and so I worked at it and I used to get up at five in the
morning, cut the meat, let the milkman and the baker bring in the

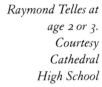

*Raymond Telles at
age 2 or 3.
Courtesy
Cathedral
High School*

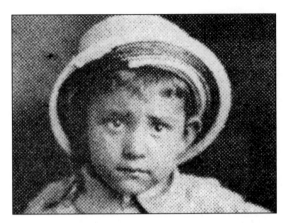

milk and bread, and then go to school." Putting their children to
work at an early age, Ramón and Angela Telles hoped to instill in
them a work ethic and a sense of responsibility. "I was taught how
to earn," Raymond Telles observes.[7]

The parents hoped to gain better futures for their sons. "Their
big ambition," Telles remembers of his parents, "was to get us out
of the barrio—get us out of the barrio not because they were
ashamed of the barrio, [but] simply because they wanted [us] to
improve; in other words, they figured that the opportunities they
didn't have they were going to give to us." Education could provide those opportunities. The Telleses prepared Raymond for
school by first sending him to a neighborhood preschool taught by
Luz Villalobos. Learning in Spanish, Raymond began to master
the art of studying. "[By] the time I went to St. Mary's to first
grade," he observes, "I already knew how to add and subtract and
divide and all that, which the other kids didn't."[8]

Although Spanish was the home language, Ramón Telles
wanted his children to learn English well (both parents knew English). Despite financial strains, he enrolled his boys in Catholic
parochial school rather than the public schools in the barrio—the
so-called "Mexican schools"—that provided inferior and limited
schooling. Besides wanting a better education for their children,
Ramón and Angela Telles also desired a Catholic education for
them. Although it was some distance from their home, the children

enrolled in the predominantly Anglo St. Mary's Elementary School in central El Paso under the direction of the Sisters of Loretto. "He never believed that because we were of Mexican ancestry that we should be confined to a particular small area in El Paso," Telles recalls of his father's desire that his children attend St. Mary's. "He felt that we belonged to the community and we should be a part of the everyday life of the community, not just in our own little area."[9]

Raymond did well at St. Mary's under the watchful eyes of the nuns. Aided by his preschool training, he achieved immediate promotion to the second grade. In seven years, St. Mary's helped mold Raymond's character. He learned, for example, to stand up for his rights among his mostly Irish American fellow students and to believe that he was just as good as the rest of them. This did not come easily at first and more than once Raymond engaged in fisticuffs to defend himself and his younger brother, Nacho, from taunting Anglo boys. He came to be respected, however, and in time formed lasting friendships with his classmates. His good friend, Richard Smith, who lived in exclusive Kern Place on the northside, often invited him to play tennis amidst opulent surroundings compared to the barrio.

Besides learning to get along with others, Raymond also received devout religious training at St. Mary's. An altar boy, he served Mass throughout his tenure at the school. "I used to come every morning from way down there in south El Paso, walk all the way down to the Immaculate [Conception Church] . . . and serve Mass, which I did for many years until I was able to afford a pair of skates. So every morning at five o'clock, here I came in my skates." St. Mary's expanded Telles's knowledge. He excelled in arithmetic and spelling and, while having some problems with English, graduated speaking it quite well and with almost no accent. Conversing in Spanish at home and English at school, he became a well-adjusted bilingual, with his languages an indispensable asset in his later work and political career.[10] Part of this acculturation or biculturation included now being addressed by the nuns as "Raymond" rather than Ramón. Among his friends he was simply called "Ray." Such Americanization of Spanish first

Freshman class picture. Raymond Telles, front row, fourth from right, The Chaparral, *1930. Courtesy Cathedral High School*

names was not uncommon among what is referred to as the Mexican American Generation.[11]

From St. Mary's, Telles continued his Catholic education by enrolling in 1929 at the all-boys Cathedral High School run by the Christian Brothers. His attendance there initially proved to be less of an economic strain on his parents since his father by the late 1920s now operated a successful taxi and transfer service, Ramón's Transfer. For *cinco centavos* or five cents, Ramón's taxi could drive you across the border to Ciudad Juárez. Those who used the taxi service were other Mexican Americans or Mexican nationals. In addition, Ramón Telles had also constructed an apartment building in south El Paso that he rented to tenants. The effects of the Great Depression by the early 1930s, however, temporarily ended Ramón's business experiment and he returned to bricklaying. Despite the need to pay tuition fees of four dollars a month at Cathedral, he remained determined that his children should receive a quality education.[12]

At Cathedral, which had been operating since the 1920s, the Christian Brothers reinforced the discipline Raymond had received at St. Mary's. Although the majority of students were Anglos (predominantly Irish Americans), some more middle-class Mexican American students also attended. Moreover, some of the more prominent families from Juárez sent their sons there. During Telles's years there (1929–1933), his fellow students included Leopoldo Villareal, who became a leading surgeon, and René Mascareñas, who became mayor of Juárez.[13]

It was at Cathedral that young Raymond began to recognize certain class distinctions. Coming from a poorer south El Paso family, he noticed that most of the other boys dressed better than he did. Still, these differences did not get in the way of his becoming integrated into the tightly knit and supportive school environment. He especially liked the esprit de corps facilitated by the small classes and small overall enrollment.[14]

Although not among the top students academically, Raymond maintained his interest in mathematics as well as becoming more proficient in English and developing a taste for history. He also became the best typist in his class and was given permission to study bookkeeping at nearby El Paso High School. Attracted to sports, he could not effectively compete in football or basketball because of his smaller stature at the time. "This friend of mine, Fred Schell, and I would go out for football," he recalls, "and, of course, we'd get pretty well banged up 'cause we were young and at that time I wasn't as big as I am now. I was rather small. We'd get all banged up and Coach Bob Carson would come and say: 'Ray and Fred, listen fellows, please do me a favor . . . why don't you go home and stay home, don't come to practice anymore.'"[15]

Not big enough for football or basketball, the two main sports, Raymond instead participated in tennis. His involvement in extracurricular activities, however, was limited because he had to work with his father after school. Nevertheless, in his junior and senior years, Raymond did participate in the Thespians and performed in school plays. These included a three-act comedy, *The Romancers,* in his junior year and "Crime Conscious" in his senior year in which he played the role of a butler. Telles remembers that he enjoyed being in these plays. He was also a member of the Pep Club and the Glee Club.[16]

Shy, Telles did not attend many of the dances cosponsored by Cathedral and Loretto Academy, the Catholic all-girls high school across town. He recalls that he and Fred Schell attended a prom at Loretto, but without dates. "We ate everything they had, but we didn't dance." He also had no girlfriends during his high school years.[17]

When Raymond graduated in 1933 from Cathedral, the humorous senior prophecies in *The Chaparral* yearbook jokingly had this to predict of his future:

> "I have not heard from Telles since we left Cathedral High," I said: "What is he doing?" "Raymond is something of a black sheep. He is supposed to be the head of a large transfer company in El Paso, but I believe that he is really a sort of racketeer or gangster." "I am certainly surprised at Raymond."

Raymond Telles's senior picture, The Chaparral, *1933. Courtesy Cathedral High School*

Telles's own assessment of his future was more to the mark. He chose as his personal senior quote the lines: "I am master of my fate. I am captain of my soul."[18]

Although deeply religious and influenced by the Christian Brothers, especially by one of his religion teachers, Brother Emil, and by his principal, Brother Benedict, Raymond did not graduate from Cathedral with any sense of a religious vocation. He notes that his best friend Fred Schell, by contrast, believed that he wanted to become a priest and tried to convince Raymond to follow the same course. Telles demurred and told Schell: "This is where we part company."[19]

Like most Mexican American youths at the time, Raymond could not even contemplate attending college, especially during the depression. Yet determined to continue his education and being pragmatic about his future, after graduating from Cathedral he enrolled at the International Business College in downtown El Paso. With his interest in mathematics and his ability to type, he prepared for a clerical career. He paid for his courses by typing and running the mimeograph machine in the evenings for businesses who contracted with the school. After completing his college work in 1935, he obtained a clerical position in the Works Progress Administration (WPA) in El Paso.[20]

In preparing for his adult life, Raymond Telles also received inspiration from his parents in other ways. They exhibited compassion for those Mexicans poorer than themselves. Ramón Telles was highly respected by the Mexicans of south El Paso who referred to him as "Don Ramón." They saw him as their leader and they often approached him with their particular problems. "He was always ready and willing to help people," Telles notes, and "he talked to us about our responsibilities to our community."[21]

His mother's example particularly affected Telles as he grew up. He recalls that neighbors called his mother "Angelita"—Little Angel: "She was always concerned with the welfare of the people in the barrio, if anything happened, why they'd call Angelita to come over and . . . if somebody got sick, why Angelita would be there to help. If there was a family fight, argument, they'd call Angelita to try to settle the problems and she would be called at all hours of the night. . . . Whenever a problem arose, why, there she was."[22]

During the depression when his mother operated the family grocery store, El Palacio, located across the street from their home, she refused to pressure customers who could not pay their bills. Instead, she provided credit for milk, bread, and *chorizo* (Mexican sausage). At one point, Angelita was feeding some thirty people out of her own home as well as providing shelter for some of them. Raymond and his brothers helped in the store and would awaken at five o'clock to help their mother. Her unselfish devotion to her neighbors eventually took its toll. She contracted double pneumonia. This weakened her heart. Although the doctor warned her not to work so hard, she continued helping others. As a result, she had a relapse and died in 1940 at the age of 45.[23]

Civic and political commitment rounded out Telles's early socialization. As a youth he displayed no personal interest in politics, but observed his father's fascination and involvement with it. "[My] dad was considered a leader in the south side," Telles notes. Heading an informal Mexican American political club during the thirties, Don Ramón negotiated the Mexican American vote with those Anglo politicians who promised improvements in El Segundo Barrio. "What organization he had was his own," Telles explains. "These people had confidence in him and he was more or less the leader and they knew that his only interest was to try to improve the conditions."[24]

Besides his barrio alignments, Don Ramón was well connected with the courthouse politicians, both Anglos and the few minor Mexican American ones. His taxi and transfer service, in fact, was located just across from the courthouse, facilitating his political ties. Telles recalls one incident in the 1930s when an Anglo politician, A. B. Poe, who had an auto dealership and was running for mayor, approached Don Ramón about securing the south side vote for his candidacy. "Mr. Poe came to my dad and said: 'Ramón, I'd like for you to support me for mayor.' My dad responded: 'I'd be glad to but first tell me what you'll do for south El Paso.'" Poe's response was apparently unsatisfactory. Don Ramón did not support him and Poe lost the election although not necessarily because of the lack of Mexican American votes. "He was a tough character," Telles notes of his father, "he didn't take guff from anyone." Ramón Telles's commitments to the barrio plus his aspirations for his older son in time combined to affect the course of Raymond's life.[25]

Shaped by his parents and the Catholic schools, Raymond Telles commenced in the 1930s a personal success story. From being a typist in the payroll department of the El Paso WPA, he worked his way up to paymaster in about two years. "[This] was an interesting situation," he remembers, "because the paymaster had to be bonded and I couldn't because I wasn't of age. I was only about nineteen or twenty years old. And we had to be bonded, but they overlooked it . . . because I was trying to do a good job for them and I did." Telles's experience with the WPA also led to admiration for Pres. Franklin Roosevelt and the New Deal, a sentiment shared by many other Mexican Americans: "Roosevelt provided a job for us . . . for me, anyway. And he provided some work for my dad on some of these government programs. So naturally . . . we thought that the man was great." In 1939 after passing a federal exam, Telles left the WPA for a better clerical position at the federal correctional institution at La Tuna, Texas, just north of El Paso. Thanks to the federal government, Telles survived the depression and emerged with a degree of occupational mobility.[26]

During this period, Telles also met his future wife, Delfina Navarro. The Navarro family was from northern Mexico and had found refuge in El Paso, as had many others, from the Mexican Revolution of 1910. Delfina's father was a contractor/carpenter who worked for local lumberyards. The family first lived in east El Paso on Manzana Street, but in time moved north of the tracks where they bought a two-story home on East California Street. Delfina attended business college where she met Raymond. She recalls that she at first didn't pay much attention to him. For one, Delfina moved in a different social circle. Her parents, unlike the Telleses, belonged to the Casino Mexicano, the most exclusive social club for Mexicans in El Paso, composed largely of prominent families who had found refuge in the border city during the Mexican revolution. Raymond began to attend some of the youth dances sponsored by the Casino and eventually he and Delfina became attracted to each other. They dated, usually going to the movies with her sister, Neomi, and Raymond's good friend, Angel Valenzuela (who later married Neomi). Delfina's parents would not allow their daughters to go out with young men by themselves. After completing business college, Delfina went to work for some financial offices in town. Delfina recalls that at first her parents were hesitant about Raymond but grew to like him and to accept him.[27]

Raymond contemplated marriage but also knew that he faced his military obligation, especially with another world war in the wind. He decided to first do his one-year service through the draft and then return to his job at La Tuna and marry Delfina. The problem was how to get drafted right away in order to get his military service over with as soon as possible. Fortunately, his father's attorney, E. B. Elfers, was also the head of the draft board in El Paso. Elfers was able to pull a few strings and Telles was drafted in February 1941. "I didn't know one end of a rifle from another," he notes.[28]

Yet being drafted into the army only accelerated Telles's personal mobility besides providing an important background for his future political career. "I was one of the first ones drafted out of El Paso," he observes, "and the war wasn't on yet." Inducted at Fort Bliss in El Paso, Telles left for Brownwood, Texas, where he joined the 132d Field Artillery of the 36th Infantry Division. "I was fortunate because most of the boys, most of the Spanish-speaking boys that went from El Paso, went to the infantry and not the artillery within the division. We were all sent to Camp Bowie in Texas. I say fortunate because it was luck to go to a field artillery and not the infantry which . . . was pretty rough, and most of our boys went into the infantry because . . . of their lack of training."[29]

At Camp Bowie, his clerical experience proved useful and he worked as a clerk in the supply battalion. Drafted as a buck private, within three months Telles achieved promotion to sergeant, an unusually rapid acceleration and, according to Telles, unheard of for a Mexican American. "But, because of my training, it really gave me the opportunity and I was there at the right time, at the right place." Three months later, with another promotion, Telles now served as a technical sergeant in charge of his own battalion supply unit.[30]

Raymond sorely missed Delfina. Moreover, after the Japanese attack on Pearl Harbor on 7 December 1941, he recognized that his military service would be extended indefinitely. He decided to get married. Before his next assignment, he returned to El Paso and married Delfina on 15 February 1942 at St. Ignatius Church on the south side.[31]

With the United States' entrance into World War II, Telles made the best of additional opportunities. Along with other high-ranking noncommissioned officers, he took the examination for Officer Candidate School (OCS) in the army air corps (which later became the air force). Telles passed and became one of four selected from his group to attend OCS in Miami. Delfina accompanied him, only to return to El Paso due to the lack of married housing facilities there. In Miami one of Telles's fellow trainees was Clark Gable, the famous movie star, who at the end of the training session threw a huge party for all the new officers. Telles remembers Gable as a nice, hardworking individual, but who, despite being in training, was still actively pursued by many of the young women in the Miami area. Successfully completing OCS, Telles graduated as a second lieutenant and was assigned to command his own squadron of new recruits at Kelly Air Force Base in San Antonio.[32]

Although not sent overseas like most other new officers, Telles notes that his original unit, the 132d Field Artillery of the 36th Division, had been shipped to the Italian front where it met with disastrous losses. Many Mexican Americans were assigned to Company E out of El Paso. One such soldier, Gabriel Navarrete, became a military hero in that battleground and would later be one of Telles's strongest political supporters among the Mexican American veterans. "I could have been part of that," Telles observes of that conflict. "I guess the good Lord was watching over me."[33]

Wedding of Delfina Navarro and Raymond Telles, 15 February 1942.
Courtesy Raymond L. Telles

Back in Texas, his bilingual abilities proved to be assets and he soon headed a newly created Latin American Division responsible for providing American-built airplanes to Latin American countries supporting the Allied cause as well as for training officers from these nations. Telles traveled to Mexico, Brazil, and other Latin American countries that were receiving U.S. military assistance. He remained in charge of this program until the end of the war. Although he had wanted to be assigned to a military theater, Telles was told that his work with the Latin Americans was indispensable. At the conclusion of World War II, he went to Mexico as a liaison officer between the now U.S. Air Force and the Mexican Air Force. By then he had been promoted to the rank of captain.[34]

Raymond Telles with officials from Paraguay,
Kelly Air Force Base, San Antonio, 1944.
Courtesy Raymond L. Telles

Raymond Telles
receiving award from
Peruvian military
official, Kelly Air Force
Base, 1944.
Courtesy
Raymond L. Telles

His assignment in Mexico turned out to involve a pair of secret missions. The first concerned Mexico's desire to obtain new shipments of American military planes which the U.S. Congress had not authorized. However, the American military, specifically the air force, decided to send twenty-five to thirty planes to Mexico without such authorization. Telles's role was to make sure the planes arrived in Mexico, were turned over to the Mexican Air Force, and were serviced. His assignment was known only by the top officials including the commanding generals of the U.S. and Mexican Air Forces and the U.S. ambassador to Mexico. No one else, as far as Telles was aware, knew of this secret shipment. He was told that if the mission were to be discovered, the air force would disavow any knowledge of it and of his involvement.[35]

The developing cold war between the United States and the Soviet Union had spilled over into Mexico and Telles's second secret mission was to determine what, if any, infiltration the Soviets had accomplished within the Mexican military. In carrying out both of these assignments, he ran into certain difficulties with the official U.S. military attaché at the U.S. embassy in Mexico City, a brigadier general. Not knowing of the secret missions and not aware of Telles's role in Mexico, the attaché confronted Telles.

"Ray, what exactly are you doing here?" he asked.

"Well, I don't know," Telles responded. "I'm supposed to be a sort of liaison between you and the Mexican military." But he could say nothing of his secret mission.

Dissatisfied with the answer, the attaché complained to the ambassador who called both men into his office. The ambassador told Telles: "The general here is complaining. You're assigned here, but he doesn't know what you're doing. In fact, I don't know what you're doing either. What's going on?"

Telles could only respond as he had earlier to the attaché. The ambassador, even though he was aware of the secret mission, was unable to divulge such information and acted out a reprimand. "He bawled me out," Telles recalls. "He went up one side and down the other."[36]

After the meeting, a disturbed Telles called the commanding general of the U.S. Air Force in Washington and reported the situation with the attaché. A month later the attaché was transferred. He was replaced by a man who this time was briefed on the secret mission. "Telles is in charge of the project," this attaché was apparently told by the commanding general. "I don't want you to bother him. Just leave him alone. Give him whatever help he asks for."[37]

Things worked out better with the new attaché, but after almost three years in Mexico, Telles felt that his efficiency was waning. He had successfully seen to the transfer of the planes and had maintained their service. He had reported on a certain although apparently not major Soviet infiltration of the Mexican military. Moreover, he had served as an aide to Gen. Dwight D. Eisenhower when the general visited Mexico City in 1946. One year later, Telles served in the same capacity when Pres. Harry Truman likewise visited Mexico. Beyond this, Telles did not know that he could do more. His request for a transfer was approved and he was reassigned to Randolph Air Force Base in Texas.[38]

Although pleased to be returning to the States, Telles nevertheless felt sorry for his successor in Mexico who, among other things, could not speak Spanish. He also was unfamiliar with certain customs among the Mexican military which involved, according to Telles, going out for drinks in midafternoon. He would often be invited by Mexican officers to join them for this socializing but always insisted that he would only do so if he could drink Coca-Cola. The Mexican officers came to accept this. But his replacement did not know that he could negotiate this drinking relationship and consequently felt that he had to compete in drinking with the Mexicans. Within six months, Telles notes, his successor became an alcoholic and had to be removed.[39]

When Telles returned to the United States he did so as a major. In his six years in the military, he received the following awards: the Legion of Merit of Mexico, the Distinguished Flying Cross of Peru, the National Order of the Southern Cross of Brazil, Colombia's Honorary Air Force Wings, the Nicaraguan Presidential Letter of Commendation, and the Medal of Merit of Aeronautics of

Mexico. In addition, he received the U.S. Army Commendation Ribbon and the American Theater Ribbon. Although once tempted to make the service his career, Telles decided to return home and civilian life in 1947. He remained in the U.S. Air Force Reserve where he was eventually promoted to colonel.[40]

Telles arrived in El Paso a changed man. Never having left the border city until drafted into the army, he, along with many other Mexican Americans, had expanded his vistas by being sent to other parts of the country as well as of the world. "My own little world was limited to this area," he recalls, "so I hadn't really gone anywhere and, therefore, this [the war] was an experience that I gained in the service, which naturally helped me to mature, helped to get me more experience, and to find out what the world was all about." Telles returned more confident of himself and of his ability to perform as well as any other American:

> I never felt less than anybody else. To me the idea was to be prepared, do a job, not only as well but better. Like when I was in the service, you know, in this supply squadron there were only three Mexican Americans and I had some preparation 'cause I had some education, the other two didn't. So I knew in my own mind that I could be as good or better than any of the others that were there, even though they were all Anglos, you know, but that didn't bother me in the least. I wanted to work and I proved it to myself that I could. In other words, there couldn't have been many others that could have been promoted to tech sergeant, for example, and they didn't. I was promoted because I was able to do the job. I was capable of doing the job and I was willing to work. So I never had a complex as far as my name being Telles and the other people's being Smith or Jones or whatever—it never bothered me at all.[41]

Richard Telles recalls that his older brother definitely returned home changed as a result of his military experiences in the war. Raymond now, according to Richard, possessed more "smarts" and had learned a great deal in the military. But, as Richard (who himself was too young to serve in World War II) further observes,

Raymond's change was consistent with similar transformations experienced by the thousands of Mexican Americans who patriotically served their country in the war. "The best thing that happened to the Mexican American," Richard concludes, "was being taken by the army. They started to learn about equal rights. If I'm going to die for my country then I want a piece of the cake."[42]

CHAPTER TWO

County Clerk

Home again, Raymond Telles resumed his accountant position at La Tuna Correctional Institution. At first he and Delfina lived in her parents' home on California Street until they built a duplex for themselves on Virginia at Nevada Street, just north of the downtown area. His father, however, had other plans for him. Mexican American participation in both city and county governments consisted only of minor token offices and community leaders believed the time had arrived to change this. Seeing in Raymond Telles an "electable" candidate, they successfully encouraged him to participate in civic affairs. Moreover, believing that returning Mexican American veterans could be key supporters in any election, Richard Telles, Raymond's more highly politicized brother, arranged to have Raymond elected as commander of a newly formed Mexican American veterans' organization.[1]

Having polished his image, and despite the obstacles of a poll tax that discriminated against Mexican American voters, community leaders, at the urging of Telles's own father, asked Raymond

29

to run for county clerk in 1948. "Why they chose the office of county clerk," Telles recalls, "I don't know, but they did." The position had been held since 1938 by P. D. Lowry, a seasoned and tough politician. Cautious by nature, Telles turned down his father's request to oppose Lowry. Yet, after a few months he had second thoughts: "I realized that I was being somewhat selfish. Selfish because of the time, effort, and sacrifices that my dad was making for our people along with the other people that followed him . . . and I knew also that in the eyes of his friends, why he had failed . . . in a sense, 'cause I hadn't accepted and they'd been look- ing for someone to put up there and push him. Dad had asked me to do one thing in my life and I had turned him down. I felt pretty bad about it." According to Richard Telles, Raymond had no choice but to accept. No one, certainly not his own sons, defied Don Ramón. "The old man was tough," Richard observed, "and Raymond dared not say no." Reluctantly, Telles agreed to become a candidate. "I never thought for a minute that I could be elected." Not expecting to win, he requested and received a year's leave of absence from his federal job. Telles never returned to La Tuna.[2]

In mid-May 1948, Telles announced his candidacy for county clerk in the 24 July Democratic Primary. Victory in the primary was tantamount to election in Democratic Texas. The *El Paso Times* noted that besides his military service and his previous employment, Telles had been active in community affairs since his return to civilian life. This included being a member of the Junior Chamber of Commerce and serving on the boards of directors of the Federal Government Employees Credit Union and the El Paso Chapter of Texas Credit Unions. He also belonged to the Catholic Knights of Columbus and had served one term as commander of the Segura-McDonald Post No. 5615 of the Veterans of Foreign Wars (VFW). "Telles," the *Times* reported, "said he plans an active campaign based on his record for business administration in and out of civilian life." Other Mexican Americans besides Telles ran for county offices in the 1948 primary, but his candidacy symbol- ized Mexican Americans' political hopes that year.[3]

Meeting Pres. Harry Truman at the El Paso train station, 1948.
Telles is third from the right.
Courtesy Raymond L. Telles

Indeed, the 1948 election inaugurated a new force in Mexican American politics in El Paso that influenced Raymond Telles's political future. Returning from a war to save democracy, Mexican American veterans—the *veteranos*—resolved to have democracy at home. Victims of discrimination before being drafted and encountering it again on their return, especially on job applications, they organized to achieve equality of opportunity for Mexican Americans in El Paso. "We came back with new ideas," veterano leader David Villa remembers. As part of their reform program they hoped to build effective Mexican American political representation in local government. They wanted to break with the older tradition referred to by historian John Higham as "received leadership" in which Anglo politicians handpicked accommodating Mexican

Americans to act as "leaders" for their community. Instead, they sought a more authentic or "internal leadership" that emanated from within the people. To achieve this, the veteranos led by Gabriel Navarrete, David Villa, and others formed the Segura-McDonald Post of the VFW, named after two Mexican Americans from El Paso killed in the war. Although prohibited from directly engaging in politics as VFW groups, as individuals they engaged in political action. When Telles announced for county clerk, the veteranos mobilized to support their fellow veteran not only because he was Mexican American, but because they believed he could do the job. "We had to make . . . a start someplace," recalls Navarrete, a school friend of Telles. "We thought Telles was the best man for that position. . . . We wanted a qualified man."[4]

Telles's campaign was overshadowed and affected by the fierce political battle waged between the *El Paso Herald-Post* and its editor, Ed Pooley, and the *Times* and its editor, W. J. Hooten. These two longtime rivals clashed over the race for the Sixteenth Congressional District, involving El Paso and parts of West Texas. The more conservative *Times* supported the incumbent, Ken Regan, who had been elected to fill out the 1946–1948 term of Congressman R. E. Thomason, now a federal judge in El Paso. The liberal *Herald-Post* countered by endorsing Woodrow Bean, a state representative from El Paso. In this contest, neither newspaper minced words.

The *Herald-Post* considered Regan unacceptable for his support of wealthy special interests such as the railroad and real estate lobbies. Pooley accused Regan of serving only the rich. "Mr. Regan is outmoded," he stressed, "he would be a 1929 thinker in a 1949 Congress—and he is a man whose main interest is special interest and not the people as a whole. He has, we think, the 1929 conception that prosperity and human happiness must trickle down from the top of the economic pyramid, rather than rise from the broad base that is the great mass of the people." Moreover, the *Herald-Post* believed Regan to have been ineffective during his tenure in Congress. Various pieces of legislation he had introduced concerning the district, including a new post office, remained stalled. He had likewise failed to prevent appropriation decreases for local military facilities. Finally, Pooley considered Regan to be too old: "He is the oldest man ever elected to Congress from this district. He is 55, and he cannot be expected to reach real leadership in the House."[5]

By contrast, Pooley lauded Bean as a "progressive," who would more accurately represent the people of the district. Bean as a state legislator had consistently voted for reform measures such as increased educational expenditures, workmen's compensation, veterans' benefits, hospital expansion, old-age assistance, tax reform, and support for labor unions. At age 31, he would have the time to rise in the House seniority system. "Bean is a progressive," Pooley concluded, "and Regan is a reactionary; . . . Bean is vigorous and Regan is inactive; . . . Bean will keep abreast of the times and Regan's ideas are set and inflexible."[6]

Editor Hooten of the *Times*, in his support of Regan, concentrated less on defending the congressman than on attacking Bean. Hooten dismissed the age issue by arguing that Bean had little legislative experience. "Congress is not a training ground, or a school," he noted. "It is where the laws of our nation are made. A man should have proved his ability before asking to be sent to Congress." Unfortunately, the *Times*, in concert with the emerging cold war spirit, charged Bean with being a "radical" because of his liberal legislative record. "If the group supporting Woodrow Bean chooses to call him a 'Progressive,'" Hooten editorialized, "it is only fair to say that a number of those who are opposed to him prefer to call him a 'Radical.'" The *Times* alleged that the supporters of Henry Wallace and his Progressive party applauded Bean's candidacy, although Hooten did not believe Bean personally supported the "red-baited" former vice president. The *Times*, however, labeled one of Bean's speechwriters, Art Leibson, a "Wallaceite." "He [Bean] has leaned to the left of center," the *Times* added.[7]

In portraying him as a "radical," Hooten observed that Bean had regularly supported pro-labor legislation such as the closed shop. In an attempt to bait Bean, the *Times* requested his views along with those of Regan regarding the controversial Taft-Hartley Act, considered antilabor because it limited the right of unions to strike. Predictably, Regan stated his support for it, while Bean diplomatically avoided the baiting by remarking that his views coincided with the *Times* editorial position on the bill reported one year earlier. At that time, the newspaper had expressed serious reservations about the fairness and efficacy of the legislation. One year later, however, the *Times* supported Taft-Hartley. An angry Hooten reported that Bean had failed to adequately respond. "A man who believes he is capable of representing the Sixteenth Congressional District in Washington," Hooten claimed, "should have the courage to state his views plainly on an issue as controversial as the Taft-Hartley Act and not resort to the age-old trick of trying to hedge by quoting parts of editorials published a year ago."[8]

While the bitter race between Bean and Regan dominated the news, Telles nonetheless profited from the controversy. The congressional campaign excited people about voting in the primary. More importantly, given the liberal-conservative division in the election, the *Herald-Post* brought Telles under its promotional wing. A supporter of Mexican Americans in El Paso, Pooley endorsed Telles. The *Herald-Post* accused the incumbent Lowry of using his office to provide favors for his friends and called on voters to replace him with Telles. "Mr. Telles will have no sideline businesses," Pooley wrote. "He will give the people a full year's work for his year's pay, and we believe he will serve the County well." The *Herald-Post*'s support provided political legitimacy to the Telles campaign, uplifted it from appearing to be only an ethnic challenge, and gave Telles access to valuable media attention. "Now the man that I owe a lot, and I'll never forget, is Mr. Ed M. Pooley," Telles states. "He endorsed me and he went all out in supporting me . . . and reporting everything that I was doing." With Pooley's aid, Telles promoted himself as a candidate who would return efficiency and a concern for ordinary people to the office of county clerk. "As part of my military service," one plank of his platform read, "I headed a Government lend-lease branch, supervising about 250 civilian employees and handling millions of dollars in equipment and materials. In three years my office saved the taxpayers several hundred thousand dollars. I am ready to bring that service to the office of county clerk."[9]

Telles pursued a twofold strategy that would also serve him well in future elections. On the one hand, he and his supporters, primarily his father's colleagues and the Mexican American veterans, built a Mexican American electoral base. Telles pragmatically avoided an open ethnic campaign that would irritate Anglos, but at the same time knew that he could not possibly win without a large Mexican American vote. Consequently, he endorsed an unpublicized ethnic movement in the barrios as his supporters tirelessly secured the Mexican American vote on the basis of ethnic loyalty. On the other hand, he campaigned as an efficient and responsible administrator with both military and civilian background. Telles recognized that he needed a certain percentage of Anglo votes north of the tracks. His strategy was neither ingenuous nor opportunistic; it was suited to his temperament and to the realistic assessment of what a candidate of his background had to do in El Paso politics. In his twofold strategy, he sought exposure to as many people as possible. As he put it: "Well, the strategy was my going out and meeting people. At that time the political campaigns were a lot different. You didn't have television, for example. We had radio, but then they had many of these political rallies. . . . [W]e'd go to Ysleta and you'd get out there and you'd sit there before several hundred people . . . and each candidate would get up and put on his little show or tell them what you had to say and try to convince them that you were better qualified than the other candidates. So most of the campaigning was done on that basis, on a personal basis."[10]

Taking advantage of these public rallies, Telles debated Lowry before the voters. "Raymond Telles, running for county clerk, is developing into one of the best crowd pleasers on the campaign circuit," the *Herald-Post* announced. At one event attended by nearly seven hundred, Telles promised that he would be a full-time official and a "friend to the public at all times." Lowry countered that he ran his office efficiently and had accumulated a profit to the taxpayers of $44,000 over 10 years. Two days later in San Elizario, in the Lower Valley, Telles questioned Lowry's budget contentions. He did not dispute the county clerk's figures, but noted that these profits resulted from registering the postwar baby boom and had nothing to do with Lowry's administrative skills. "The real test will lie in the years ahead, when the boom subsides," Telles predicted. "That is when you will need a proven administrator to take care of the clerk's office. I can do it, as my background proves." To allay fears that he would make a clean sweep of the county clerk's office if elected, Telles emphasized that he ran against Lowry only and not the county workers. A *Herald-Post* reporter favorably compared Telles's performance with that of Bean's: "The two men youngest in years are stealing the show from the rest of the field on the El Paso County campaign circuit. The older candidates receive a courteous response when they finish their talks. But the big ovations are reserved for 31-year-old Woodrow W. Bean and 32-year-old Raymond L. Telles, Jr." Two days before the election, both Telles and Bean received an enthusiastic reception from a Mexican American crowd at Armijo Park in south El Paso. Telles appealed to the voters to go to the polls and reminded them that he was one of them. "I know you are behind me," he said. "Most of you have known me since I was a small child." A reporter observed that Telles had to personally quiet the audience to get them to listen to a Mexican American spokesman for Lowry.[11]

Besides exposure at open rallies, Telles carried his campaign to the public in other ways. He walked door-to-door passing out his campaign literature and took advantage of radio interview programs. He managed to buy some radio ads, especially on the less costly Juárez stations, just prior to the primary. To reach as many people as possible, he recorded his announcements in both English and Spanish. "English if it was directed to the north side of town," he explains, "and Spanish to the other side." In this personal effort, his wife, Delfina, assisted him by making phone calls, contacting friends, and accompanying her husband to the various political rallies. She recalls that at some of these rallies, she and other women prepared and served tamales to those in attendance.[12]

Yet the real key to Telles's campaign lay in its organization headed by Richard Telles. More like his father than the other two sons, Richard inherited Don Ramón's astute political instincts and

combative personality. Richard masterminded a strategy for getting Mexican Americans to the polls. A nonveteran, Richard,
unlike Raymond, had gone into business for himself and operated
both a cantina and a vending company (jukeboxes, pinball machines, and cigarettes) serving bars in south and southeast El Paso.
Through his business contacts and as Democratic precinct chairman for the south side, Richard organized an informal political
network that in later years would come to be referred to by his
political enemies as the "organization." "We started developing an
organization that made white folks begin to recognize the strength
of the Mexican American people," Richard notes. The 1948 campaign allowed him the opportunity to apply his political talents in
the service of his older brother. "You had to be tough in those days
to exist," Richard recalls of this first political battle.[13]

Spearheaded by Richard Telles and the veteranos, the Telles
movement diligently organized Mexican American voters concentrated in the south portions of the city. Months prior to the primary, Telles supporters had urged them to pay their poll taxes.
This was not necessarily easy since the poll tax was $1.75, a prohib-
itive fee for many poor Mexican Americans. To offset what they
considered a form of political discrimination (the poll tax was
declared unconstitutional in 1966), Richard and the veteranos col-
lected money that they advanced to those unable to pay the tax.
They, for example, promoted dances and raffles as fund-raisers.
Mexican American merchants excited by the Telles candidacy
donated freely to the campaign. "We did everything we had to
do," Richard explains. "We even went to Juárez." Well-known in
the neighboring Mexican border city, Richard had few problems
acquiring financial support from sympathetic politicians there. In
addition, he borrowed money from friends and acquaintances.
With these funds, Mexican Americans unable to pay the poll tax
out of their own pockets could now do so. As Richard correctly
notes, there was nothing illegal in the action. He skillfully utilized
the cantinas of south El Paso, where Mexican American workers
congregated, as organizing centers for the dispensation of funds
and mobilization of volunteers. He also took advantage of the fact

that the county recorder, Charles Terrazas, was a friend. In charge of recording poll taxes, Terrazas provided Richard and his supporters poll tax registration forms and allowed them to turn in the forms past the registration deadline. Determined not to be excluded from political representation by the poll tax, Richard and the veteranos believed in the righteousness of their cause. Moreover, they pointed out that the practice of providing voters with poll tax money had been originally conceived by Anglo politicians. "But they did it on the north side," recalls David Villa, "why shouldn't we do it?"[14]

Whether accepting money for the poll tax or paying it from their own wages, Mexican Americans by the thousands registered to vote. As Raymond Telles puts it: "I think it was a lot of enthusiasm that was generated because, well, here's the first Mexican American that dares to run for office and, my gosh, we're going to help him." Telles did not appeal to them on the basis of ethnic loyalty. The name Telles was enough. Richard recounts: "The thing that got us together more than anything else was pride." As the main Mexican American candidate, Telles coalesced the south-side electorate around him. "At that time it was just me," he states. "So everybody concentrated on me, everybody. It was just like a little revolution. . . . People getting registered."[15]

Not initially considered a major threat to Lowry, Telles by the end of the campaign forced the county clerk on the defensive. To regain momentum, Lowry unfortunately stooped to race-baiting. He went on the radio and told the listening public: "I want the people of El Paso to know two things about me and my opposition. First of all, his name is *Ramón Telles*. And my name is P. D. Lowry. He's a *Mexican* and I'm Scotch-Irish." Lowry, according to Richard Telles, believed that many Anglos did not know Raymond was a Mexican and hence wanted to set the record straight and appeal to anti-Mexican sentiment in the city. Indeed, Telles began to receive crank phone calls opposing his candidacy. Lowry also accused Telles's father of being a thief and a smuggler. While the racial issue had not gone unnoticed during the campaign, it had remained "under the table"—to use Raymond Telles's words—until Lowry's radio appeals. Telles refused to fall into Lowry's trap

by engaging in an ethnic war of words and cautioned his supporters to disregard the county clerk's tactics. If anything, Telles
believed that Lowry's racial statements would offend certain Anglos. "They [the Lowry campaign] found that they couldn't fight
my brother on anything," Richard notes, "because Raymond had
a clean record. He was clean from the word 'go.'" Moreover,
Lowry's desperate efforts served to redouble Mexican American
support for Telles. They felt insulted by Lowry's comments since
Telles was an American citizen who had participated in the war.
"Are we going to let a guy [Lowry] like this belittle us?" veterano
Navarrete asked other Mexican Americans.[16]

To ensure that Lowry's tactics did not work and to leave nothing for granted, the Telles campaign intensified its activities the day
before the election. Political ads were placed in both the *Herald-Post*
and the *Times*. Stressing Telles's military and administrative records,
one ad read: "A yes for Raymond L. Telles Means A Working And
Full Time County Clerk," while another stated: "Raymond L.
Telles Jr. 100% Qualified. From A Private To a Major . . . U.S. Air
Force." The *Herald-Post* predicted a record turnout of at least
24,000 and reminded its readers to vote for Telles. "He is just the
sort of man we need in public life here on the Border." The newspaper, however, conceded a "nip-and-tuck affair" between Telles
and Lowry. The *Times*, for its part, endorsed no local candidates
but expressed no enthusiasm for Telles. Instead, its support for the
conservative Regan in the congressional race indirectly favored the
similarly conservative Lowry.[17]

On election day, Telles supporters worked to deliver the Mexican American vote. Richard Telles and the veteranos appointed
coordinators in each southside district who in turn supervised
individual precinct captains. Under this command setup, the
Telles people phoned registered voters, walked door-to-door, and
drove voters lacking transportation to the polls. Dr. Raymond
Gardea noted that he and about twenty-five to forty other Mexican
American students in Sigma Iota Pi Fraternity at the local Texas
Western College volunteered to get the vote out. "I was out there
at all the precincts still shaking hands," Raymond Telles recalls his

own election-day activities, "and when I got through that evening I was tired and to be honest about it, I felt a little bit discouraged, you know, 'cause I just felt that it wasn't going to happen." The afternoon *Herald-Post,* based on unofficial and incomplete returns, reported Telles trailing Lowry by 12 votes, though Telles was "showing surprising strength in all sections of the county."[18]

Realizing that it would be hours before the complete returns came in, Telles went home to bed. At midnight, his father called and informed his son that the votes remained close and he should go to election headquarters in the city-county building. "You're very close," he repeated, "you'd better come on down 'cause they're liable to steal the election from you." Since Lowry as county clerk possessed responsibility for election returns, the Telles people had in fact already taken precautions against vote tampering by designating their own observers at each precinct. They also kept a watchful eye on Lowry and followed him everywhere election evening. According to Telles, "P. D. got real furious." With still incomplete returns, the *Times* reported next morning that Telles trailed Lowry 3,203 to 3,045. The Telles-Lowry race produced the most excitement and was far from being over. "None of the complete boxes were from south El Paso precincts," the *Times* observed, "counted upon by Telles to swell his total vote." Telles remembers the anxiety of waiting: "Well, it wasn't until twenty-four hours later, 'cause the counting lasted from that evening until the following evening around 10 or 11 o'clock at night. . . . I kept getting closer and closer to him till finally it came to the last box, but I felt pretty good 'cause the last box was coming from one of my precincts."[19]

The last box, Precinct 1, came in. Telles had only a 22-vote lead. Fortunately for him, Precinct 1—Alamo School in south El Paso—voted 563 for Telles to only 23 for Lowry. The final tabulation recorded 9,341 for Telles and 8,778 for Lowry—a margin of only 563 votes and exactly the number Telles had received from Precinct 1. Telles won with 51.55 percent of the vote in a record turnout. His supporters broke into a demonstration. "Everybody was happy," he recollects about his victory, "I was happy. It was something I had not anticipated. Didn't even think it would happen, but it did; of course, my father and his friends were all very happy." Acknowledging that the 1948 election marked the political baptism for many young Mexican Americans, Gabriel Navarrete observed that Telles's election as county clerk signaled the first step in the Mexican American quest for political representation and status in El Paso. "It was just a miracle that it happened," Richard Telles modestly recalls of the election, "but it happened."[20]

The strategy succeeded and Mexican Americans in El Paso had flexed their political muscles. Beginning with an ethnic base, Telles realized that he had to bring out Mexican American voters and accumulate sizable margins in the south El Paso and Lower Valley communities where important Mexican American enclaves existed. This he accomplished. In the eight south El Paso precincts (1 through 6 plus 29 and 30) Telles amassed an overwhelming 79.85 percent of the vote—2,489 to Lowry's 628. In the five Lower Valley precincts that he carried, Telles likewise won big. His margin in these precincts (including the communities of Ysleta, Socorro, San Elizario, and Fabens) was 1,211 to Lowry's 663. In Precinct 47, Fabens School, Telles buried Lowry 194 to 9. Combining his south El Paso tally with his Lower Valley one, Telles accrued a lead over Lowry of 3,700 to 1,291. The incumbent, despite winning a majority of precincts (29 to 21) could not overcome Telles's substantial margins in the predominantly Mexican American neighborhoods.[21]

Yet Telles won by also doing well in the northern precincts. He ran close to Lowry in predominantly Anglo or mixed neighborhoods. In not a single precinct did Lowry duplicate the type of landslide vote that Telles acquired in the southern precincts. In the 29 precincts won by Lowry, Telles gained a surprising 40.32 percent of the vote. His good showing here clearly made a substantial contribution to his success. As he had admitted early in the campaign, he could not win by only carrying the Mexican American vote. In defeat, however, Lowry incorrectly claimed that only the Mexican American vote had defeated him and threw suspicion on the large margins that Telles received in south El Paso:

I was defeated by the Spanish American vote. It seems peculiar that at San Elizario (Pct. 47), I should get only 9 votes when I had at least five workers there and in Pct. 1 (Alamo School) I should get only 23 votes out of 623 cast. However, I am not contesting. I'm not a cry-baby.[22]

By contrast, Telles accepted his victory graciously and appealed for unity. "This is one of the happiest moments of my life," he exclaimed, adding:

I want to thank the thousands of friends and supporters who have made it possible for me to take over the management of the office of county clerk. I am particularly grateful that the support that I have received should come from every part of the county. I see it as the finest demonstration of cooperation between all communities that has been shown in El Paso in recent years.

I have pledged myself to conducting a friendly and efficient office as county clerk. I shall not fail in my promise to devote my entire time to the office to which I have been elected. The citizens of this county will be watching closely my conduct in office during the next two years. They will not be disappointed.[23]

In the hotly contested congressional race, Woodrow Bean lost to Regan 25,372 to 17,609 in the district but managed to win in El Paso County by more than 4,000 votes with strong support from Mexican Americans. Unlike Telles, Bean won not only in southern precincts, but in northern ones as well. His ability to attract moderate and liberal voters in the northern precincts may have assisted Telles's important vote tallies in these neighborhoods. Although disappointed at Bean's loss, the *Herald-Post* expressed pleasure at Telles's election. "Congratulations to Raymond Telles on winning the county clerk's post," Pooley wrote in a post-election editorial. "This developed into the toughest and most thrilling race of the campaign. Mr. Telles never lost his good humor, nor his courtesy, and he is to be congratulated not only on his victory but on the manner thereof. He will be an excellent county clerk."[24]

Raymond Telles served as county clerk from 1948 to 1957, being reelected four times. Recognized as an unbeatable incumbent, he faced no challengers during this period. In nine years, he turned in an unblemished performance as an administrator and matured as a civic figure in El Paso. As county clerk, he ran an efficient operation. He modernized facilities that had been plagued, among other things, by rats. In 1952, he reported the net earnings of his office over three years to be $87,147 as compared to $30,439 accumulated by his predecessor over 11 years. Telles consistently stayed within his budget. Fulfilling his campaign promise to be open to the public, he personally conducted his business in a front office where he could greet all who came for assistance. His open-door policy sometimes exceeded the normal workweek. "A lot of times I was called up on Saturdays or Sundays," he recalls. "Somebody had to have a birth certificate for a good reason whatever it was and I'd go out there and issue it to them." Telles vacated his office only once. In May 1951 he reported to active duty as a major with the air force when the United States intervened in Korea. He went to Korea in early 1952. There he served as executive officer of the Sixty-seventh Tactical Reconnaissance Group and was awarded a Bronze Star. He returned in September of 1952 and resumed his duties as county clerk. During his absence, he still kept abreast of his office by leaving his wife, Delfina, in charge on a nonsalaried basis.[25]

Telles recalls that when he was called back into the service he believed he would have to resign his position as county clerk. The county attorney informed him that this was not necessary and Telles arranged for Delfina to cover his duties for him. "We were never criticized for that," he notes. "People felt we were doing the job." This was obviously the case and Telles was reelected without opposition while serving in Korea. During his absence, he not only received the good news of his reelection but of the birth of his first child, Cynthia Ann. In 1955 his second daughter, Patricia, was born.[26]

Besides his duties as county clerk, Telles, for both personal and political reasons, plunged into community service affecting both

Mexican Americans and Anglos. He held high offices in civic organizations such as the Boy Scouts, the Government Employees Credit Union, the Rio Grande Girl Scout Council, the El Paso Tuberculosis Association, the El Paso Boys Club, Our Lady's Youth Center, and the Southwestern Sun Carnival Association. He also joined the Junior Chamber of Commerce and the El Paso Chamber of Commerce. In 1955 the Cancer Crusade named Telles as its chairman. That same year he became the commissioner of Little League. Although not an active member of the League of United Latin American Citizens (LULAC), Telles knew its leaders and supported their welfare causes. His main association with Mexican Americans continued to be his participation in the VFW. This well-rounded civic life satisfied Telles's affinity for people and his need to be involved with others, while at the same time increasing his political contacts.[27]

Telles as county clerk shunned involvement in the often heated world of El Paso politics. He avoided taking sides between contending liberal and conservative factions of the Democratic party. Instead, he wished to be considered above partisan politics. "My approach was: 'I'm a friend of everybody,' " he explains.

> I tried to impress people with the fact that I was not really a politician, that I was a friend of the people and I used that term many, many times, you know: "I'm not a politician really." I said: "I'm a friend of the people." And I worked on that basis. It didn't make any difference to me whether your name was Torres or Smith, or if you were black. . . . I mean I was friendly to everybody and I tried to provide services to everybody. In other words, I made no distinctions.[28]

Two political trends influenced Telles's future political career. One involved the liberal-conservative split in El Paso politics. Not openly ideological, this division consisted of differences between a conservative business elite—whom Pooley referred to as the "Kingmakers"—and a loose coalition of more liberal small businessmen, professionals, and union leaders that desired to democratize local politics. Both in name adhered to the Democratic party. Yet the Kingmakers in fact more closely resembled Republicans in political philosophy, while the liberals shared greater affinity with the national Democratic party, although not on all issues. Indeed, liberalism in El Paso generally meant supporting a more open political process in local government and greater attention by local government to the needs of the "masses" in the city. The conservative-liberal dichotomy also contained an ethnic dimension. Most Mexican Americans supported liberal rather than conservative political candidates. Finally, El Paso's local political wars were fought out in the pages of the conservative *El Paso Times* and the more liberal *El Paso Herald-Post*.[29]

During the late 1940s and early 1950s this liberal-conservative split affected both city and county elections. In 1949, for example, the *Times* endorsed the incumbent mayor, Dan Ponder, over ex-mayor Dan Duke, a union man. The *Herald-Post* did not support either candidate, but suggested that Ponder, despite some important achievements, had been slow in pursuing various improvements in south El Paso. Duke won a decisive victory. Two years later, conservatives and liberals clashed even more. Self-made fast-food millionaire, Fred Hervey, challenged Duke. In a bitter campaign, Hervey upset Duke by more than 3,000 votes. In 1953 Hervey faced no opposition. Pooley consistently opposed Hervey's administration and referred to it as a "succession of crackpot schemes," while sarcastically saying of Hervey's policies: "Our hamburger merchant is handing out baloney, and we wonder if he thinks anybody is falling for that sort of stuff."[30]

Disappointed at Duke's loss, Pooley and the *Herald-Post* hoped to regain liberal momentum. The first opportunity came with the congressional election of 1954. In an editorial entitled "Mr. Regan and El Paso," Pooley charged the incumbent congressman again with ineffectiveness and with being a puppet of the Kingmakers. Pooley observed that Regan's opponent, J. T. Rutherford, would not be controlled by El Paso's business elite. In one of the district's closest elections, Rutherford won by only 152 votes. A relieved *Herald-Post* expressed great satisfaction and contrasted Rutherford's populism with that of the Kingmakers. "He made a marvelous campaign," it said of Rutherford. "It was 'poor boy' politicking at its best. He had no large sum of money at his disposal in contrast to his opponent, whose 8,175 votes in El Paso County more than likely cost the Kingmakers a dollar or more each."[31]

Inspired by Rutherford's election, Pooley and the liberals looked toward 1955 and the city elections. Fred Hervey chose not to run for a third term and instead supported, along with the Kingmakers, a conservative ticket headed by a relatively unknown businessman, W. T. Misenhimer. The liberals countered with Dan Duke again. The *Herald-Post* dismissed Misenhimer as simply a tool of Hervey and the Kingmakers. "A little gang of willful men," Pooley suggested of Misenhimer's selection, "gathered in the penthouse of the Hilton Hotel and decided they would select the man who would be El Paso's next mayor. Not being able to convince their top choice to accept, they finally out of desperation turned to the 'Unknown One'—Misenhimer, who agreed to 'love, honor, obey and bow down to the Kingmakers.'" Pooley derisively labeled the Misenhimer ticket as the "Hervey–Kingmakers–Unknown One ticket."[32]

During the campaign, Pooley and Duke concentrated on attacking Hervey. They noted that, despite an increase in city revenues, Hervey had been slow in financing much-needed improvements. Public pressure, according to the *Herald-Post*, finally forced the mayor into supporting reforms such as repairing and repaving streets. Pooley accused Hervey of being insensitive to the needs of the people: "He confused the operation of a city with the conduct of a hamburger business." Pooley warned readers that Misenhimer would be no different. On the other hand, Duke pledged more efficient city services, especially to the poorer sections of south and east El Paso.[33]

The *Times* responded to Pooley's and Duke's charges against Hervey by claiming that the mayor had accomplished more than previous administrations. It charged Duke with inciting racial tensions by claiming that Hervey had not aided Mexican Americans. The *Times* reminded Mexican Americans of Hervey's street improvements and of other changes in south El Paso. "Can you remember when the south side was a community with muddy streets before the street and alley program was started and the ugly tenements which gave way to Frontera Park and swimming pool?" Hervey, according to the *Times*, had also hired more Mexican Americans into responsible city jobs. Labeling Duke a politician who supported a spoils system, Hooten called on voters to elect a business administration. "The real issue in this political campaign," he claimed, "is whether El Paso is going to be run as a business—or as a private political property."[34]

The election proved to be a disaster for Pooley, Duke, and the liberals. Misenhimer rolled to an almost two-to-one victory: 11,049 votes to Duke's 5,646. He carried 37 out of 45 precincts. Duke won only eight precincts and even had problems on the liberal south side. In Precinct 12, Bowie High School, he won by just two votes and in Precinct 13, Alamo School, he lost by 21 votes. Not excited by the campaign and with some community leaders favoring Misenhimer, many Mexican Americans refused to vote at all. The *Herald-Post* congratulated the winner, but observed that his access to substantially more campaign money had proved to be the difference. The Duke fiasco made Pooley and the liberals, who had lost three straight city elections, rethink their strategy and look for a more electable candidate in 1957. They turned to Raymond Telles.[35]

The election of Telles as county clerk in 1948 had increased the political involvement of Mexican Americans who continued to run and to be elected to lesser county positions, such as justice of the peace. More importantly, they accelerated their total political presence. Mexican Americans formed supportive blocs for particular mayoral candidates, both liberal and conservative. In the 1949 election, for example, a group of Mexican American leaders headed by Modesto Gómez, long-time LULAC activist, endorsed the candidacy of incumbent mayor Dan Ponder over Dan Duke. In both the 1950 and 1954 congressional elections, Richard Telles organized south-side voters on behalf of liberal candidates. In turn, Anglo politicians began to include Mexican Americans on their campaign staffs and on their tickets. In the 1951 city elections, Fred Hervey chose Mexican American businessman Ernest Ponce as one of his aldermanic candidates. Although not a community activist, Ponce was perceived by the Hervey campaign as their "ethnic" candidate. To counter Ponce, as alderman for parks and recreation, the opposing ticket of Dan Duke selected Moises Flores. Ponce easily defeated Flores and swept into office with Hervey. As the liberal candidate, Flores won only nine precincts, all on the south side. In the heated 1955 campaign, both the Duke and Misenhimer tickets included Mexican Americans. Ponce ran with Misenhimer for reelection to a third term as alderman, while Art Maya campaigned with Duke. Ponce easily won in the Misenhimer landslide. Besides seeking local offices, Mexican Americans challenged for state ones as well. Lawyer Paul Andow carried Mexican American hopes into the 1952 race for state representative. His campaign slogan read: "Young Enough to be Progressive . . . Old Enough to be Reliable." Andow finished third in a slate of six candidates, carrying eight south-side precincts.[36]

Mexican Americans strengthened their political presence in El Paso by likewise increasing their registered voters. In 1951, LULAC Ladies Council 9 won the sweepstakes poll tax contest involving civic clubs. "We have been getting out the vote every year," declared Mrs. Joseph Rey, chairwoman, "but it has been a telephone campaign in the past. This is the first time we actually sold poll tax receipts. Most of the women in our club work days but get on the phone in the evening. Friday night we will take poll lists and begin calling to get the voters to the polls."[37]

Mexican American political activity pressured the Hervey administration in the early 1950s to carry out certain improvements on the south side and to appoint Mexican Americans to relatively high city positions. These included Joe Herrera as city clerk, Nick Pérez as city engineer, and Dr. M. D. Hornedo as city-county health director. Luciano Santoscoy, LULAC council president at the time, recalls that LULAC presented Hervey with a petition from south-side residents that helped convince the mayor to pave some sidewalks and streets in the area.[38]

More acculturated, more educated, and slightly more occupationally mobile than their parents, young Mexican American adults aspired for full integration into the civic life of El Paso. Repulsed in their attempt to secure authentic political representation by electing candidates from their own ranks, they particularly hoped for electoral success. Yet they desired to play politics on their own terms and not as an ethnic group manipulated by either Anglo or Mexican American politicos as in the past. "It is about time," wrote activist Aurora Mata in 1955 as one of Telles's key supporters in 1948,

> that the citizens of El Paso awaken to the fact that the Latin American people of South and East El Paso are intelligent enough to decide any issue on the facts or their sincere beliefs. Some of these citizens (including myself) may not speak English fluently, or understand it in general, but they can decide an issue for their own betterment, for the city, and for problems that exist solely in their neighborhood. They are not a herd of cows that have to be led by so-called leaders.[39]

Believing that their time had come to achieve the highest elective office in El Paso, Mexican Americans turned to Raymond Telles in 1957.

CHAPTER THREE

The 1957
Election

In 1955 Mexican American leaders (excluding Ramón Telles who had died in 1952) encouraged Telles to run for mayor. He, however, expressed ambivalence about his prospects as a Mexican American candidate and concluded that the political climate was not right. "In other words," he recalls, "for me to win, there had to be a very special issue, an issue whereby people would vote against the other group and not necessarily in favor of me. So at the time I decided that the issue wasn't there." One year later, Mexican Americans again assessed their chances of winning the 1957 mayoral election. "We were hungry to get one of our men to be a mayor of the city," "Kiko" Hernández of LULAC explains. "We had that burning desire. You know when people have that burning desire that's when they get hot." The veteranos, LULAC officials such as Alfonso Kennard, Richard Telles, and others, again approached Telles. "I wanted to see Raymond become mayor," LULAC member "Lelo" Jacques notes, "because I knew that if Raymond would be mayor, that some day Raymond would be a congressman."[1]

51

Telles agreed this time. He now believed conditions to be propitious for two reasons. First, the city's annexation of the Lower Valley, downriver from El Paso, initiated by the Hervey administration and concluded by the incumbent one, had produced anger and discontent among Lower Valley residents. This protest might effectively be organized into a solid bloc of voters. "See, many people were unhappy with the administration because they annexed the Valley without consulting with the people of the Valley," Telles recounts; "that was one issue." Second, Mayor Tom Rogers had not been elected by the voters and probably was vulnerable. Rogers, a businessman, had been appointed mayor by the city council in consultation with the Kingmakers who convinced Misenhimer to resign following his election citing health reasons. "I decided at that time that it was possible [to win]," Telles remembers his decision. "I knew it wasn't going to be easy. I knew it was going to take a lot of money, which I didn't have, and it was going to be very difficult getting people to run with me." Telles had lingering trepidation, but by late 1956 he was in the race.[2]

Albert Armendáriz, one of the few Mexican American lawyers and a past national president of LULAC, recalls being present at a strategy meeting with Telles in November 1956. One important discussion concerned getting Mexican Americans to pay their poll taxes. Telles was the perfect candidate to excite Mexican American voters. If they would not vote for him, they would not vote for anyone else. Yet their vote would not be enough. He would, as in 1948, need some Anglo support. His supporters, such as Armendáriz, believed Telles could appeal to Anglos and not threaten them. "We chose him because he's diplomatic-looking; he's light-skinned; he's impeccable; he speaks perfect English," Armendáriz notes. "I mean here was a qualified Mexican American to be mayor. And that was the thing we were looking for. We didn't want to postulate a person for mayor that was going to be rejected on the basis: 'Hey, he's not qualified.'"[3]

The issue of qualifications, of course, had been a particularly aggravating one for Mexican Americans in El Paso and elsewhere. They had nurtured and cultivated Telles so that when the time came to advance him for mayor, no one could question his credentials. If El Paso accepted Telles, it would accept other qualified Mexican Americans in politics as well as in other fields. "You have to understand the basis for Raymond Telles in this community," Armendáriz stresses:

> Our leadership had been told time after time again that the reason we didn't go up was because we weren't qualified. And this was a term that was not only used against us but it hurt. It ruffled our dignity as a group. It was a system; it was a *modus operandi*: "you're not qualified." And in doing this for Raymond we were able to . . . present an entirely qualified candidate. None of us were foolish enough to believe that we could put Raymond Telles in as anything—dogcatcher—if we did not sway a substantial section of the Anglo community to vote for him. This was basic in our thinking.[4]

To test the reaction of the Kingmakers to his candidacy, Telles decided to pay a visit to Sam Young, the president of El Paso National Bank and the most powerful of the Kingmakers. Young at first was polite and friendly and wanted to know what he could do for the county clerk. Telles told him that he had decided to run for mayor against Tom Rogers. He recalls that at that point, Young almost fell out of his chair and proceeded to become agitated. "You must be crazy," he angrily told Telles. "No Mexican will ever be mayor of El Paso." The unannounced candidate responded: "Well, maybe so, but I'm still going to run."[5]

In the race, Telles decided not to formally announce his candidacy until close to the filing deadline of 23 January for the early March primary. First he had to gather a ticket of aldermanic candidates and plot a campaign strategy. In the meantime rumors abounded concerning a Telles candidacy. The *Times* noted that the Rogers administration, despite having alienated some voters, would definitely campaign and should be reelected. Editor Hooten hinted at a Telles challenge, but downplayed the county clerk's experience and public exposure. "And remember," he told his readers:

With representatives of Veterans of Foreign Wars in El Paso, circa late 1950s.
Telles, back row, third from the left.
Gabriel Navarrete, back row, first from the left.
Courtesy Raymond L. Telles

no public official could possibly conduct his office in such a way that he would please everyone; that is, if he has to make decisions affecting the public. A county clerk or district clerk escapes direct contact with the general public because no public decisions are made by him. But that is not so when it comes to the sheriff, the County judge, or County Commissioner and, most certainly, the mayor and aldermen.[6]

The *Times* rated Rogers's performance as mayor highly and warmly welcomed his formal announcement for election on 12 January. The Rogers team included incumbent Alderman Ponce seeking a fourth term. Still noting persistent rumors of a Telles ticket, Hooten wrote: "As far as this newspaper is concerned it hopes that Telles goes ahead and announces his candidacy or definitely says he will not be in the race. Rumors become tiresome after awhile." Whether Telles ran or not, however, the *Times* supported Rogers. As two scholars later wrote of Hooten and the Kingmakers, whom they referred to as the "influentials": "The influentials all agreed that the election of a Spanish-name person as mayor of El Paso was acceptable in principle, and that it should and would happen, but they were not prepared to have it happen in their lifetime."[7]

In organizing his campaign, Telles began with a strong family foundation including his wife, Delfina, and his two brothers: Joe, who ran the family business, Ramón's Transfer, and, of course, Richard. The youngest Telles brother, a key to Raymond's election in 1948, would prove invaluable again through his political and business contacts among Mexican Americans. Missing, of course, was Don Ramón. Telles felt sad and apprehensive that his father would not be around to help him as in the 1948 campaign. Outside of family, the veteranos stood ready to literally march once more for Telles. A more active LULAC through both the men's and women's councils could assist in registering voters. At the *Herald-Post*, Telles knew he could count on Pooley. With these initial supporters and advisors, he planned his strategy.

As in 1948, he started with a Mexican American base. He could not possibly win without their vote, not only south of the tracks, but also in the central districts now housing many who had made it out of the barrio. They would have to be mobilized and registered to pay their poll taxes. Moreover, with the Lower Valley annexation, Telles could expand his base to include this area, numbering at least 50 percent Mexican Americans, that he had carried in the 1948 county election. If he could win big in Mexican American precincts and in the Lower Valley, Telles knew he had a chance to be mayor. The overall strategy, according to Richard Telles, and one he believes is still applicable to contemporary campaigns, was to hold the Mexican American vote together while splitting the Anglo vote.[8]

Nevertheless, both Raymond and Richard likewise recognized, as in 1948, that they could not run an openly ethnic campaign. Such a strategy would undoubtedly cause a backlash among

Anglo voters. Raymond Telles did not deceive himself. He understood that most Anglos would perceive him as a Mexican American candidate regardless of what he did. But if he accented the ethnic appeal, even more Anglos would register to vote just to keep a Mexican out of the mayor's office. He would also risk the chance of scaring away those Anglo liberals and moderates he hoped to attract. "I realized," he recalls, "that the odds were very much against me because my name was Telles." Hence, he decided on a "People's Ticket" campaign. He would stress that he stood for El Paso's common man against the elite Kingmakers. Telles, the populist, could appeal to both Mexican Americans and Anglos. Finally, he would conduct an issues-oriented campaign, while relying on Pooley's *Herald-Post* to aggressively and polemically attack the Rogers ticket. "See, the name of the ticket was the People's Ticket," Telles explains, "and we wanted to give the impression that we were dealing with all the people not just one sector, 'cause if we had ever given the impression that we were there representing only the Mexican Americans we would've been killed. I mean, we would've never gotten anywhere."[9]

Telles and his supporters concluded that three objectives had to be achieved in carrying out their strategy. They had to first select a ticket that would complement the populist theme and help Telles with Anglo voters. Second, Telles, as in 1948, would run a nonethnic "public" campaign stressing his administrative background and proposals for reforming city government. Finally, Richard Telles, as he had done nine years before, would operate an ethnic "nonpublic" campaign. He would mobilize the Mexican American vote and turn it out on election day. The Telles campaign would consequently possess different personalities in different areas of El Paso. The candidate would appeal as an American populist throughout the city, while in the southern precincts Richard would ensure that ethnic loyalty tied Mexican Americans to his brother. As in 1948, this strategy did not translate into a split personality nor opportunism on Telles's part. He personally found no comfort in running as an ethnic candidate and believed it more appropriate to present himself as an American citizen who believed in a democratic form of city government. At the same time, he astutely realized that to win, his supporters had to specifically organize Mexican Americans.

The selection of a ticket proved to be no easy task. Few Anglos desired to run on a ticket headed by a Mexican American. Telles hoped to entice businessmen candidates to counter Rogers's emphasis on a business approach to city government. He recalls: "So I tried gaining these men, but I found it was not possible. 'Cause I approached several of them and several of them said yes and then a couple of days later they came back and said sorry." Telles became aware that many of these potential running mates had been intimidated by local bankers—part of the Kingmakers—who threatened these businessmen that they would not renegotiate their loans if they dared to join Telles's ticket. Consequently, he turned to citizens with less prominent business backgrounds. Ernest Craigo, an insurance man, agreed to be on the ticket. Telles had known Craigo in the air force reserve. Jack White, service manager for a local auto dealer, also joined the team. More importantly, Telles acquired the services of Ted Bender, a local television and radio personality, and Ralph Seitsinger, a Lower Valley businessman. El Pasoans knew Bender as the "friendly weatherman" and could identify with him. His daily radio and television appearances would indirectly publicize the campaign. "I didn't think that there was a chance of losing," Bender remembers his optimism in working with Telles. Seitsinger turned down being on the ticket at first, but agreed to locate a suitable candidate from the Lower Valley. He could not. "Don't get on that Mexican ticket," he heard Lower Valley bankers tell potential candidates. Unable to find a running mate for Telles, Seitsinger joined the ticket himself. Telles had wanted him all along: "I knew Ralph was very popular in the Lower Valley, I knew that he had a lot of friends." Seitsinger likewise proved an asset by contributing $3,000 to the campaign and by getting a Lower Valley contractor, Joe Yarborough, to substantially fund Telles's efforts. Telles complemented the Seitsinger selection by naming Ray Marantz as campaign manager. Marantz possessed no political experience, but had Lower Valley contacts through his insurance business.[10]

Having chosen a ticket and having organized a campaign structure and strategy, Telles formally announced on 22 January, one day before the filing deadline. "Ours is the People's Ticket," his announcement emphasized, "and if elected, it will be a City Government by the people and for the people of El Paso. We shall bow to no bosses." Telles pledged that his administration would more effectively represent all the people of the city. "Ours will be an administration that serves no special interest or particular area; rather we propose to offer conscientious service to the entire community." Telles reminded voters that as county clerk he had fulfilled all of his campaign promises. He concluded, borrowing from Lincoln:

> If I am elected mayor of El Paso, I will again promise the people of El Paso that I will be a full-time mayor, and a fair, honest, progressive, efficient and courteous administrator.
>
> We realize the tremendous responsibility that will face us the coming two years, if elected, but we are confident that with the help of God and the assistance of the people of the city of El Paso that we will have a successful administration of the people, by the people and for the people.[11]

Although a declared candidate, Telles still had to put up a $2,500 registration fee which at that point in the campaign he lacked. He had twenty-four hours to raise the money. However, the county clerk recalled that some weeks before, a highly prominent businessman, MacIntosh Murchison, had told Telles that if he needed campaign money, he could be of help. He went to see Murchison and reminded him of his promise. "I remember," he told the candidate. "How much do you need?" Telles mentioned the $2,500. The businessman said, "No problem." He took out his checkbook and made out a check to Telles for that amount. As Telles reached to take it, Murchison said, "Don't forget me and my associates when we need to have our taxes reduced." Without hesitation, Telles refused to accept the check. "Thank you very much for your offer," he told Murchison. "All I can offer you is good government." Telles left the meeting dejected and believing that his campaign was stillborn due to the absence of the registration fee. He walked slowly toward the corner of Kansas and San Antonio Streets in the downtown section. It was at this point that he recalls a "miracle" occurring:

> Like an angel from heaven, there across the street was a wonderful person, K. B. Ivey, walking towards me. He was a friend of mine from the Lower Valley and a leader among the farmers in the area. When he walked up to me, he said, "Raymond, you look as though you have lost your last friend. What is the problem?" This was approximately four o'clock in the afternoon, twenty-four hours to the deadline the next day to register and put up the filing fee. I told Mr. Ivey my problem. He said, "Raymond, you meet me at this same corner tomorrow at four o'clock in the afternoon." That would be an hour prior to the deadline. I went on and told my four council candidates that I had not been able to raise the $2,500, and I also told them about meeting Mr. K. B. Ivey and that he had told me to meet him the next day. I further said that I was not too optimistic about being able to raise the $2,500 by the deadline. I had nothing to lose so the next afternoon at four o'clock I went to the corner of Kansas and San Antonio Streets. I waited a few minutes, not really thinking that I would see Mr. Ivey. However, much to my surprise, I saw him walking toward me. The next thing I knew, he was pulling money bills from all of his pockets, enough to cover the $2,500 filing fee. In doing so, Mr. Ivey said very emphatically: "This money comes from your friends in the Lower Valley, and we are not asking for anything except good government." I told him: "I promise you and our friends that you can count on good and honest government." So from there, I rushed to the city clerk's office and paid our filing fee. This is how close we came to not running for office.[12]

Once formally in the race, Telles swiftly mobilized to register Mexican American voters before the poll tax deadline on the last day of January. His announcement for office triggered a frenzy of activity. From campaign headquarters in the basement of the First

National Building on North Oregon Street, the Telles organization plotted its voter registration drive. "It was . . . a big dark basement where we'd get together," Telles recalls; "It was dreary, and
it wasn't very pleasant. But we'd meet there every day and then
we'd decide, well now, you're going this way and I'm going that
way." Campaign manager Marantz remembers that they stressed
registering those Mexican American who had never voted, including the elderly. Telles estimated that he would need at least 90 percent of the Mexican American vote.[13]

The registration pursued various methods. LULAC members,
although barred by their constitution from endorsing political candidates as an organization, assisted Telles by feverishly selling poll
tax receipts to Mexican Americans. LULAC Council 132, for
example, hosted a dance and charged the price of a poll tax for
admission. It also sponsored films at the Colón Theatre in south El
Paso where admission was payment of a poll tax. LULAC members likewise set up poll tax booths in a variety of locations in
downtown, south, and southeast El Paso as well as going door-to-
door. They got Mexican American merchants and grocers to
become deputy registrars and to sell poll tax receipts in their stores.
Francisco "Kiko" Hernández, who sold them at his drugstore in
southeast El Paso, remembers that he and other LULAC members
helped those who could not pay their poll taxes by finding work
for them: "We did everything we could to get people to pay their
poll taxes." Members further went to barrio churches and sold poll
taxes after Sunday Masses. Conrad Ramírez, a LULAC official at
the time, recalls receiving much support in southeast El Paso from
Los Compadres, a community group of Mexican Americans working out of Our Lady of Light Church and led by people such as
Mrs. Frank Maldonado. In all, LULAC sold 4,378 poll tax receipts
and won the Junior Chamber of Commerce Poll Tax Contest. At
Smeltertown, where hundreds of Mexican Americans worked at
the ASARCO plant, Mexican American officers of the Mine, Mill,
and Smelter Union registered voters for Telles. *El Continental*, the
city's Spanish-language newspaper, aided Telles's voter registration
drive by alerting voters to where they could pay their poll taxes.

Finally, Richard Telles and his veterano allies, as in 1948, gathered poor Mexican Americans and assembled a formidable bloc of pro-Telles voters. (See Chapter Four.)[14]

Telles's candidacy electrified the Mexican American community and, with the untiring work of supporters, led to a significant increase in Mexican American registration. "We had a saleable product," Albert Armendáriz notes. "I'd say that probably 98 percent of the Mexicans really wanted to do something for the man," LULACer "Lelo" Jacques recounts. "They saw him probably as an image for the Mexicanos." Total registered voters in the city numbered 42,542 as compared to 40,635 in 1956 and only 30,412 in 1955. The most impressive increase occurred in Mexican American areas. In the south and southeast, Precincts 10 through 19, some 1,627 more voters registered than in 1956. Poll tax increases in eight south El Paso precincts accounted for more than 65 percent of the 2,196 gain in 36 precincts experiencing increases. Precinct 12, Bowie High School, went from 285 voters to 461; Precinct 13, Alamo School, went from 439 to 668; Precinct 16, Beall School, went from 720 to 908; and Precinct 17, Jefferson High School, from 1,084 to 1,508. This excitement was poignantly brought to Telles's attention when one day he encountered an old blind Mexican American man being led by a young boy who appeared to be his grandson. Thinking that they were lost, Telles inquired if they needed help. The boy replied: "Could you please tell us where my grandfather can register to vote? He's a citizen and he wants to vote for Raymond Telles. He's never voted before."[15]

By contrast, registration in Anglo or mixed neighborhoods went up only slightly or not at all. Seven north El Paso precincts increased only from 4,225 to 4,241. In 14 northeast precincts, with mostly Anglo voters, registration went only from 11,626 to 12,104. Combining the number of registered voters in predominantly Mexican American precincts, Telles could begin with a reliable base of 7,960. The balance to win would have to come from Mexican Americans in northern precincts, a minority of Anglo voters, and the Lower Valley. The total number of Lower Valley voters was 9,515. *Herald-Post* columnist Dr. B.U.L. Conner observed that the rival *Times*—which he referred to as the "Morning Crimes"—had suggested that some El Pasoans had been illegally registered. "It is doubtful that the Morning Crimes will file charges against a women's service club or voter," he noted. "Besides, the Crimes is trying to scare people because it is scared its ticket is going to be beaten in the City election."[16]

Having registered voters, the Telles "public" campaign now developed issues to stimulate interest in him, differentiate his ticket from Rogers's, and showcase his grasp of city government. Telles chiefly emphasized that his administration would be oriented toward people, as compared to the elitism of the Rogers administration. As mayor, his door as well as those of his aldermen would always be open to the public. "We have no bosses but the people," his platform read. No secret meetings would be held to decide any policy: "The people will be advised regularly as to what is happening in their municipal affairs." A Telles administration would solicit the views of all El Pasoans by regularly scheduling neighborhood meetings. "There is a fundamental difference between the two tickets," Ted Bender stressed. "It is that we of the People's Ticket believe in the rights of the individual while members of the opposition seem to believe that their strength comes from wealth." Telles hammered at the democratic approach of his ticket. A vote for him was a vote for "government of the people, for the people and by the people." The candidate emphasized that the Lower Valley annexation only reinforced the undemocratic character of the previous administration that paid little heed to the wishes of the people and the needs of poorer neighborhoods. "It was a good political issue," Marantz recalls of the Lower Valley.[17]

On specific issues, Telles distanced himself from Rogers. He pledged to expand the parks and recreation department and provide much-needed new facilities throughout the city. He criticized the lack of adequately paved streets, street lighting, and flood control. The administration, he noted, pleaded a lack of revenue for its inability to control flooding, but at the same time had provided exorbitant funding for a new Ascarate golf facility. "Flood control rather than golf courses deserves priority," Telles told voters, "so that you will not have to be in constant fear for your homes and families when a few clouds start to build up in your area." He further called for expanded garbage collection and for improving El Paso International Airport. On the often heated subject of the police, the county clerk promised utmost courtesy on the part of officers and a more efficient force. He revealed that under the Rogers administration, auto traffic injuries increased 11 percent and deaths 20 percent. Telles objected to Rogers's use of roadblocks to check on traffic and drinking violations. Roadblocks had not lessened these occurrences and instead harassed citizens. "Roadblocks are for the apprehension of criminals," his platform noted, "and the City Police will use roadblocks for this purpose only." Radar traps to catch speeding drivers would be discarded and the public warned about the use of radar. Prevention, not punishment, should be the aim of such devices. "There is no substitute for the patrolling policeman," Telles concluded. "Radar is an assistance, but increased conscientious and courteous activity of police patrols will control excessive speeds, accidents, and deaths."[18]

Financially, Telles explained that he could better administer city hall. He possessed administrative experience in both the military and as county clerk where he had proven to be a frugal and honest administrator. "Taxation is necessary for good government," he pointed out, "but excessive or unfair taxation of groups or individuals is un-American." He insisted that he would study all city accounting procedures "to find and enforce a system to stop the fraudulent loss of thousands of dollars to the taxpayer." He further downplayed the Rogers administration's acquisition of an "A" credit rating for the sale of municipal bonds, contending that improved business property and continued home construction rather than the administration had increased the valuation of the city and made it eligible for the rating. Telles criticized Rogers for waiting until 1957 to secure the rating when it could have done so earlier. The delay resulted in the city's having to pay higher interest for a bond issue recently approved by the voters. Rogers's financial ineptness, he continued, had cut the city's general fund in half and forced the city to have an overdraft of $800,000.[19]

Besides running a financially solvent administration, Telles pledged that he would employ long-range professional planning to meet the city's growing needs. His council, for example, would make a thorough engineering study to determine drainage inadequacies. An inspection system would be organized to specify necessary street repairs. An origins-destination traffic survey would be made to calculate the efficiency of one-way streets. Telles contrasted his plans with the lack of foresight by Rogers who had not even published an election platform. Telles insisted that he could do a better job and appealed to the voters to elect him and his entire ticket.[20]

Lacking a large campaign fund, he carried his issues in person to the voters while Rogers made use of television. "I would go to a building, for example," Telles remembers, "one of these office buildings, like the El Paso National Bank with 20 floors, I would walk every floor and go and visit with the people. I'd walk all over the Lower Valley and walk over the areas in El Paso that I thought were very vulnerable." He told people that he wanted to be their mayor and that he hoped they would give him the opportunity to do so. Telles and his ticket had opportunities to discuss issues at numerous candidates' meetings organized by social clubs including Mexican American ones. At the meetings, the candidates, along with those from the Rogers ticket, proclaimed their platform and commented on issues. Telles encountered, as expected, close scrutiny and pressure at Anglo-sponsored assemblies. Opponents circulated preplanned questions before he spoke hoping to embarrass the county clerk. "I was always concerned about it," he recalls, "but I felt that I got along pretty good, and that my aldermen, even though they were inexperienced and young, they did very well."[21]

The tables were turned, however, when both tickets attended evening rallies in south El Paso or in the Lower Valley—Telles territory. Unlike Rogers, who could only speak in English, Telles addressed these gatherings in both English and Spanish. While he resisted an open ethnic campaign, his use of Spanish served both as a form of communication with Mexican Americans and as an ethnic

Telles with El Paso Herald-Post *editor, Ed Pooley, 1957.*
Courtesy El Paso Herald-Post

symbol. He had to be bilingual to reach different sectors and generations of the Mexican American community. "I didn't want the people that didn't know too much English—I didn't want them to be left out—and, secondly, I had to be careful because a lot of the younger people then at that time, they felt that well, he's insulting me by talking to me in Spanish. I had to relate to both groups." In south El Paso, in addition to his general platform, he promised to

improve depressed housing conditions especially in the old tenements and to possibly eradicate some of them. "And just improving conditions in general down there, for example, the canal, the
paving of streets . . . down there it was a mess; when it rained it
was just a sea of mud, you know. So that's one thing that I
promised that I would do, pave streets down there and we did."
Such promises and Telles's appearance in the barrios produced
much emotion from his supporters. "People were very excited
about Raymond," Albert Armendáriz recalls.[22]

Telles formulated issues, campaigned hard, and emerged as a
serious threat to the incumbent administration and to the Kingmakers. "They [the Rogers ticket] never thought we'd give them a
battle," Telles explains. "Of course, they had all the money behind
them and all the big businessmen and so forth. So they never
thought we would put up much of a battle. But as the campaign
went on, they began to realize that they were in a political battle."[23]

Tom Rogers and his ticket (composed of Ernest Ponce, Hal
Dean, Dick Fletcher, and Bob Kolliner) avoided making a direct
issue of Telles's ethnic background. Like other Anglo political and
business leaders, they feared that overt racial animosity could only
harm the border city's economy, so dependent on Mexican labor
from both sides of the border and on commercial and tourist relations with Mexico. Ethnicity, moreover, was circumscribed by
Ponce's being on the ticket. Instead, the Rogers campaign replaced
ethnicity with what Eisinger in his study of white resistance to
black rule in Detroit and Atlanta refers to as "neutral-sounding
criteria of evaluation that function in effect as code words, mask-
ing unacceptable modes of thought and expression for both users
and their audience." As such, Rogers concentrated on the virtues
and accomplishments of his administration and on portraying his
opponent as totally inexperienced for the job. Rogers ran not as a
politician, but as a businessman who brought experience, stability,
and efficiency to the city. As the general manager of the Con-
sumer's Ice & Fuel Company and as a former president of the
chamber of commerce, Rogers insisted that he, more than Telles,

knew about management and business. Dr. Judson F. Williams, a past dean of Texas Western College in El Paso and a vice president of the prominent White House Department Store, directed the incumbent's campaign. "The administration of Mayor Rogers and his ticket has been marked by progress," Williams announced. "I feel that this progress can be best continued by the election of the Rogers team."[24]

Both Rogers and Williams continually emphasized that only a businessman could bring financial solvency to El Paso. Rogers, they noted, had obtained the city's "A" credit rating from New York investment brokers to expedite the $3.8 million worth of bonds obtained in 1956. This rating would attract new industries. Rogers also boasted that the 1957–58 municipal budget would be less than the previous year's without affecting services. He warned, however, that financial stability could be endangered if voters elected an inexperienced nonbusinessman such as Telles. By contrast, businessmen dominated the Rogers administration. "El Paso is most fortunate in having businessmen of this caliber willing to continue in office and get the job done," manager Williams stated:

> They are experienced, honest and capable. They do not and will not dodge issues and they will make the decisions, which is [sic] very important to a growing city, such as El Paso. It has been proven by the actions of Mayor Rogers and his council, that they favor no special groups at any time and that their actions are taken for the good of the entire community.[25]

Rogers admitted that not all of his decisions had been uniformly popular but claimed important accomplishments. Parks and recreation centers had been improved and new ones commenced, including Frontera Park in south El Paso. New flood control projects would soon be instituted. The police department had been improved and raises provided for both policemen and firemen. Alderman Robert Kolliner, in charge of police and fire, believed that such increases had made El Paso competitive with other Southwestern cities. He also defended police roadblocks to

*Telles with members of the People's Ticket after the 1957 election.
(From left to right): Ernest Craigo, Ralph Seitsinger,
Ted Bender, and Jack White.*
Courtesy El Paso Times

check on unlicensed drivers; roadblocks and the use of radar had made El Paso a safer city. Dismissing criticism concerning Lower Valley annexation, the ticket countered that the area had gained in services. In all, the Rogers team praised their accomplishments and pledged to bring responsible, planned growth to El Paso. This could only be done, however, by experienced businessmen. "The city of El Paso is business, big business," Rogers told a television audience, "a $7 million business annually. Unless we have a guide in the form of a comprehensive plan on a long-range basis, we can get into serious trouble in our municipal operation."[26]

Rogers accused the challenger of being unprepared to be mayor on several counts. First, Telles lacked financial experience. The incumbent criticized Telles for suggesting that an origin-destination traffic survey would only cost seven or eight thousand dollars. Rogers estimated it at a minimum of $85,000. "Any experienced businessman would know that a survey of such scope would cost many thousands of dollars," he stressed. Telles's problem, the mayor observed, lay in his county clerk position that provided no real experience in high finance. "The city of El Paso is big business," he reiterated, "and for that reason we should not talk about what goes on in the County Clerk's office, but what goes on in the Mayor's office." Hence, he hinted that Telles, if elected, would harm El Paso's economy.[27]

The mayor's emphasis on business experience resembles what Eisinger discovered of white opposition to black rule in Atlanta. By defining the administrative job in business terms, whites by definition excluded blacks from serious political consideration since whites dominated the business world. The same held true for El Paso. "Naturally enough," Eisinger further concluded:

> perhaps, white elites projected their own values onto a conception of the mayorality, but by elevating managerial experience to a position of primacy, they established a narrow notion of the range of functions of the elected political executive. That such a role might include political leadership—mobilizing, innovating, symbolizing, mediating—was scarcely admitted. . . . The analysis of the neutral-sounding standard as a code word is lent credence by the fact that few blacks could possibly meet it, for blacks have generally been denied major managerial roles in government and business.[28]

Besides charging that he lacked business experience, the Rogers campaign painted the county clerk as being devoid of character. The incumbent particularly jumped on Telles's charge of the administration's fraudulent loss of taxpayers' money. He accused him of irresponsibility by resorting to such tactics. Alderman Fletcher challenged Telles to prove the charge and noted that he had made an "irresponsible slur on the honesty of City employees."

The challenger responded by producing records of a $19,000 shortage in city license bureau funds and a $3,000 shortage in police court funds. Rogers dismissed such evidence and commented that the first shortage had occurred before he took office and the second was in the courts. He called, instead, for Telles to apologize to city employees.[29]

The Rogers campaign attempted to cast further doubts about Telles's candidacy. Alderman Kolliner, for example, suggested that Telles's opposition to police roadblocks indicated that the county clerk was soft on law and order issues. "We are happy to have our opponents so definitely opposed to strict law enforcement," he added. Rogers also claimed that Telles was "not his own man," but simply a puppet of Ed Pooley and the *Herald-Post*. "It is no secret that the editor of the afternoon newspaper wants to run the city," Kolliner charged. "Why doesn't he run himself instead of getting candidates who are ready to front for him." Rogers further indicted the Telles ticket for crass opportunism. He called the People's Ticket platform nothing but a collection of words, promises, and clichés. "At every political rally which we have attended," he said, "the opposition has cagily adopted [sic] their platform to mean whatever they thought it would take to please the people in that particular precinct." The real "People's Ticket," Rogers insisted, was his own and not Telles's.[30]

Finally, the mayor called his opponent unresponsive to the voters by refusing to engage in a debate on television. Telles replied that nothing could be debated since only the People's Ticket had a platform. Rogers disagreed and offered to pay for the entire airtime if Telles changed his mind. The *Times* suggested that Telles was afraid of embarrassing himself in front of thousands of viewers. "Why so reluctant?" it asked. "Is it because he might show when caught with his guard down, how little he knows about the city's business?"[31]

The race, while fierce, was tame by El Paso political standards, but only because both sides could rely on their newspaper support for the more hard-hitting issues. The 1957 mayoral election only intensified the Pooley-Hooten rivalry. The editors wrote what the

Raymond Telles, right, and Richard Telles, left, circa late 1950s. Unidentified person in center. Courtesy Raymond L. Telles

candidates chose not to say in public. Consequently, the newspapers proved to be valuable assets to each ticket. Telles especially relied on the *Herald-Post* since he did not have the resources Rogers possessed for television exposure. "If Pooley did not defend our ticket," Telles's campaign manager observed, "there would not be a line written on our behalf." Telles recalls that many businessmen threatened to curtail their advertisements in the *Herald-Post* because of Pooley's support of the People's Ticket. Luciano Santoscoy, who worked at the large Popular Department Store run by the Schwartz family, notes that one prominent El Paso contractor advised Albert Schwartz, an official of the store, to cancel his advertisement in the *Herald-Post* because of the Pooley-Telles relationship. Pooley shied away, however, from being a visible part of Telles's inner circle to protect the candidate from charges of being his puppet. Nevertheless, the *Herald-Post* editor provided Telles with visibility and an outlet for his platform. Moreover, Pooley relentlessly attacked Rogers and the Kingmakers. "Pooley [was] a type of man that he did what he thought was right, what he wanted to do," Telles fondly remembers.

There was no way in the world that he would ever consider me as a puppet because he didn't, you know, he knew that I had a mind of my own, but he liked what I had done in the past and he didn't like that other bunch because of what they had done . . . like annexing the Lower Valley. In other words, he felt they were taking too much for granted. That they were powerful and that they could do anything. Well, he figured it was time somebody had to fight them all the way. He fought . . . he had some very bad times . . . because of that. These people gave him a very bad time.[32]

Pooley, however, relished the struggle. *Time* magazine said of him and the *Herald-Post*: "Under Editor Ed Pooley, a Tabasco-tempered maverick who has run the paper for 20 of his 59 years, the *Herald* has earned Texas-wide renown as an ardent defender of underdogs, whom Pooley, in deference to the border city's heavy Spanish-speaking population, invariably calls Juan Smiths. On their behalf, Pooley, one of U.S. journalism's last curmudgeons, wages daily war on the 's.o.b.'s', his all-embracing designation for city officials, cops, the opposition El Paso *Times* . . . and any other non-Juan who incurs Pooley's ire."[33]

Following Telles's announcement to run for mayor, Pooley quickly editorialized his endorsement. He categorized the Telles ticket as a group of successful and competent Americans. Independent men, they would not be controlled by the Kingmakers.

There are no strings attached to any of them. All are independent Americans with minds of their own.

Not one will find it necessary to rise from his seat in the Council Chamber, face west [towards the downtown business and financial section], and bow three times before casting his vote. Nor will the five of them have to have a secret meeting before the Council session, face west, bow three times, and await instructions on how to vote tomorrow.

They are free men. They are Americans. They can run our city as an American city should be run.[34]

The editor's own campaign strategy consisted of attacking the incumbent's ticket as puppets of the Kingmakers, of representing only the wealthy, and of being antidemocratic. Rogers, Pooley contended, had been handpicked by the Kingmakers in 1955 to succeed Misenhimer. "This is an important election," he stressed. "It will decide whether the people or the bosses shall be in control at City Hall, and whether there shall be a government of, by, and for the people of El Paso, or a government of, by, and for the bosses." As the candidate of the rich, the mayor had twice as much money for the campaign as did the county clerk. Two weeks before the election, Pooley publicized figures revealing Rogers had spent $5,284.04 to Telles's $3,019.68. Rogers had received more contributions and in larger sums with individual contributions averaging $100.00 compared to $41.50 for Telles. Powerful and rich, Rogers and the Kingmakers, Pooley charged, had taken government away from the people.[35]

Pooley specifically criticized Rogers's ineptness in governing El Paso. He debunked the mayor's image as an efficient manager of the city's finances. For example, he had not completed construction of a new city-county building because, Pooley suggested, of the city's $800,000 overdraft. Moreover, his administration had displayed "immature judgment" in administrating the city budget. After two years in office, the administration had less money than when it started. "There's the financial record of the 'businessman' we have been told about," Pooley concluded. The fiery editor likewise ridiculed Rogers's pledge to reduce the 1957–58 budget. The reduction would amount to less than 1 percent of the previous budget and would still be almost 27 percent more than the budget Rogers had inherited. The proposed token cut Pooley credited to the Telles challenge: "[T]hank you, Mr. Telles, for what you have been able to do as a candidate—reverse a trend and lower a budget. We know that when you are mayor there'll be more lowering."[36]

In scathing articles and editorials, Pooley also accused the Rogers administration of allowing police inefficiency and abuse. Injuries from traffic accidents in 1956 had increased 11.8 percent and traffic deaths had gone up 25 percent. El Paso's traffic deaths were four times the national average. The administration's road-blocks had clearly failed. "Policemen who should be out patrolling and preventing deaths," Pooley stated, "are pulling out those tick-ets that bring in the revenues." In addition, Pooley blamed the police department for improprieties concerning wrecking service. Both the Hervey and Rogers administrations, according to the edi-tor, had contracted with Curly's Wrecking Service even though the owner possessed a police record in Waco before moving to El Paso. Moreover, the police department abused its contract with Curly's by calling it to tow cars at every opportunity, whether because of accidents or for overparking. In return, the department received a 25 percent rebate from the service on charges imposed on citizens. Drivers often complained of poor service and damage to their cars by Curly's. The Rogers administration distanced itself from the issue during the campaign, but Pooley believed this would not fool the voters. "Curly is one of the biggest loads the Kingmakers' ticket is carrying, but we don't think quieting him down during the election campaign is going to make the people forget the disgraceful things the police aided him in doing and that the Rogers administration renewed his contract."[37]

The editor highlighted a particular incident during the cam-paign that further suggested police abuses. Isidro R. Fernández drove his car into a storm sewer ditch one evening. He claimed that the ditch had been improperly marked and that he had remained there after the accident to wait for his lawyer so he could demand payment from the city. However, the police arrived and, according to eyewitnesses interviewed by the *Herald-Post*, proceeded to beat up Fernández, handcuff him, and drag him out of the ditch by using a cable from one of Curly's wreckers. Police charged Fernández with drunkenness and use of abusive language. "What will be the next outrage committed by El Paso police?" Pooley edi-torialized the following day. He noted that it took nine hours before the chief of police even knew about the incident. "Why it took six policemen and Curly's wrecker to get one man—drunk or sober—out of a ditch is a little too complicated for us," Pooley wrote. "Ah! Such big, bold efficient lawmen!" This example emphasized the shortcomings of the police and their disregard for the rights of citizens. The fact that Fernández was a Mexican American was, of course, not lost on some readers. The police abused their responsibilities because the city lacked leadership. "The El Paso Police Force is a shame and a disgrace," Pooley concluded, "it needs leadership and discipline. It needs leaders who are able to keep the rowdies in line, strong men who can clean up the mess so that the good officers on the Force can keep their self-respect."[38]

City services had also suffered under the current administration, according to Pooley. The city council, for example, had raised garbage fees and yet provided less frequent pick-up service than before. Two weeks before the election Pooley effectively published a series of photographic editorials showing unpaved streets, inadequate drainage in certain neighborhoods, and unkempt parks. "Yes voters, this is an El Paso street," one caption read:

> It is one of the accomplishments of the Rogers "team." This is the 3700 block of Raynor Street. Alderman Dean has been in charge of it [streets] for four years, but maybe he hasn't discovered it yet. If you go to take a look at it, drive slowly to save your tires and your car. Not even Alderman Kolliner [in charge of police] would chase a bus along this one.[39]

The Kingmakers might have been upset over the photo editorials, but Pooley believed they had good reason to be: "The Rogers 'team' has nothing to brag about so it bewails the photos that point out its failures."[40]

Finally, the newspaper aided the Telles campaign by publishing anti-Rogers and pro-Telles letters to the editor. The writers, many of them Mexican Americans, seconded Pooley's contentions of poor city services by the Rogers administration. Reflecting Lower Valley discontent over annexation, Hubert H. Heath, for example, called on El Pasoans to vote the Rogers ticket out of office: "The owners of the 30 square miles of farmland, grabbed by the ruthless bunch in power, should be out working to defeat those responsible and should bill the entire area showing how these people are being bled to carry the bond load of the city, from which they draw not the slightest benefit in any way whatsoever." Letters likewise castigated Rogers for governing only for the rich. José Patino wrote: "We all know that Mr. Rogers and his Kingmakers will keep on favoring the areas where only people of high social and economic position live. They will keep on neglecting the areas of the city where there has never been sewer service, bus service, and other things." And Jesús B. Ochoa, Jr., urged voters to shed their apathy and recognize that the selfish interest of El Paso's establishment hurt the common person:

> I am convinced that the Rogers ticket is for the worse. I will go further. I am convinced that they, as businessmen, have not the city's and the people's interest in mind, but their own.
>
> Now, if the people of El Paso elect this bunch to serve another term, El Paso will remain what it has been up to date, a hick town; a hick town that is experiencing so many growing pains, that it is too undecided to know what to do about the administration that have been put in office by the Sapmakers—I can call them Kingmakers no longer. To do so would be to give too much undue credit to too many people who control the town through money, without giving a thought to the people who make it possible for them to have their power. I speak of the poor dope who is the lackadaisical and too preoccupied type of person who will not give more than a passing thought to the people who are placed in office, not by himself, but by his superiors, the Sapmakers.[41]

Rejecting Rogers, writers to the *Herald-Post* lauded Telles. Carmelita A. Pomeroy stressed the county clerk's experience. "I feel that Raymond L. Telles has the capabilities to give us the best government and appoint the best men to administer its political affairs." E. L. Forti noted his character: "He is a model man, a leader, an official of merit, a gentleman, a distinguished officer of the U.S. Air Force." R. C. Coppenbarger contrasted Telles's independence with Rogers's ties to the Kingmakers: "To me a strong administration is one that goes in there with no strings attached but goes in for the interest of everyone concerned big or small. This is the People's Ticket." And E. A. Gonzales saw in the challenger's campaign a new start for El Paso: "Youth and ability are taking over and you, Mr. and Mrs. El Paso, have the power at your command. May you choose wisely and compare, and you will see the People's Ticket headed by Raymond L. Telles, Jr., will save our El Paso."[42]

Over at the *Times*, editor Hooten responded to Pooley's anti-Rogers campaign by his own attacks on Telles. "There followed one of the roughest and toughest campaigns in the history of El Paso," Hooten wrote later in his memoirs. "The candidates, Rogers and Telles, never said particularly unkind things about each other, but the *Times* and the *Herald-Post* fought each other tooth and toenail." Hooten concentrated on three charges: (1) Telles's lack of experience; (2) his campaign tactics; and (3) his character. Like Rogers, Hooten did not directly refer to Telles's ethnicity, but instead used code words—"experience," "character"— that cast doubts on Telles's abilities and indirectly on that of all Mexican Americans. In the first case, Hooten contrasted the mayor's business career and his two years in office with the challenger's lack of business experience and what the editor considered his minor administrative duties as county clerk. "Let's nail down the phony claim that Raymond Telles has been something special as a county clerk," he stated in a front-page editorial entitled "Exploding a Myth." According to the editor, a county clerk could take little credit for increased revenues since that simply depended on the level of recordings. Being county clerk required few financial abilities. "Raymond Telles has been a conscientious county clerk," he conceded, "but there is nothing in that job or in his other so-called executive background to qualify him for the job of mayor of a city the size of El Paso."[43]

Hooten warned voters that they would be taking chances with their tax dollars if they elected Telles. In an editorial, "It's YOUR Money—Be Careful of It," he incited citizens' financial fears by suggesting that Telles could not be trusted to administer the bond money for city improvements approved by the voters. "Now the question before those same voters," he put the issue, "is who will have the responsibility of spending that $3,829,000? The men who have worked on the plans, who have had long experience behind them, or a group gathered under the 'P-for-Pooley' ticket?" Telles was a "very nice young man," he patronizingly concluded, but he had no business running for mayor.[44]

Hooten additionally portrayed Telles as a scheming politician, who would do anything to become mayor. He was, of course, only Pooley's puppet. The *Herald-Post* editor pulled all the strings for what Hooten referred to as the "P-for-Pooley ticket." Hooten turned the tables on Pooley's sarcastic castigation of the mayor's dependence on the Kingmakers by writing: "If elected, all that Telles and the men on his ticket will be expected to do three times a day will be to rise and bow three times to the North before making a decision. North is the direction from the City Hall of that certain newspaper editor's office." Hooten considered Telles to be nothing better than a "political opportunist." He deceived voters by empty promises. His championing of a "people's government" only disguised his dearth of ideas about running city government: "The entire 'P-for-Pooley' ticket ought to be defeated because its members have nothing constructive to offer. A negative group is negative at the beginning and it would be negative in the end." Devoid of a concrete program, Telles relied on appeals to ethnic loyalty and to constructing a political machine, he implied. Never openly raising the "Mexican issue," Hooten instead suggested that Mexican Americans in south El Paso might foolishly disregard what Rogers had done for them and vote emotionally and "blindly, as a bloc" for Telles.[45]

Hooten indirectly warned the Telles "machine" and alerted the "public" to its "tactics" by publicizing the stiff penalties for illegal use of poll taxes. Hooten feared that during the intense drive in January to sell poll taxes that many persons probably paid their $1.75 illegally. If they did, they could be sentenced to between two and five years. The *Times* reminded voters that only citizens who had lived in Texas for one year and in the county for six months could vote in the March primary. Moreover, any persons voting more than once could be fined up to $500. Anyone inciting a "riot" within a mile of the polls could be fined up to $1,000. No doubt with Telles's Mexican American supporters in mind, the *Times* warned that any assistance at the polls had to be conducted only in English. Anyone using a language other than English could be fined up to $500 and receive a jail term of one year. Finally, buying votes or lending money for poll taxes was illegal and carried a fine up to $500.[46]

Inexperienced and opportunistic, Telles in Hooten's eyes further lacked character. Hooten believed that Telles during the campaign had shown himself to be careless and irresponsible in his accusations against Rogers. Moreover, the challenger had displayed unethical standards by his platform's charge of fraudulent financial losses on the part of the Rogers administration. Hooten challenged Telles to prove this and if not to apologize. Dismissing the candidate's evidence as deceptions, Hooten wrote: "You have to go back a long way in El Paso's history to find anything as politically disgusting as the stunt a candidate for the office of mayor, Raymond Telles, tried to get away with." Hooten likewise attacked Telles for being weak and for attacking those who did not believe in strict law enforcement as well as unruly elements. The *Times* alleged, for example, that candidate Ted Bender had not only caused an accident, but had fled the scene. "Police late Saturday were seeking Theodore Robert (Ted) Bender, television personality and candidate for alderman in the Raymond Telles Jr. slate," the *Times* reported, "for 'changing the course of direction and causing an accident' and for 'leaving the scene of an accident.'" Bender, in the *Times* account, had hit the car of Mrs. Susana Torres and, after giving her his name and license, had left. Mrs. Torres then reported the accident to the police. However, three days later the *Times* had to retract its story after Bender complained and provided contrary evidence. Bender had not left the scene of the accident. Claiming not to have known all the details when the *Times* first broke the story, Hooten admitted that a police officer had been present at the accident but had failed to make a report.

Hooten further disclosed that he had publicized the incident because of Bender's involvement in the campaign.[47]

Besides the Bender article, the *Times* reported that police, after arresting a Lower Valley man, Ramón Frescas, for drunkenness, had been confronted by forty to fifty youths, apparently Mexican Americans, who chanted, "Things will be different when Ray Telles is elected." Citing this as evidence, Hooten in his election eve assessment of the two mayoral candidates wrote of Telles: "Those who would benefit most from a policy of loose police enforcement are loudest in their cry of 'Wait until Telles is elected. Things will be different then.'" And, in an example of irresponsible journalism, Hooten in his daily "Everyday Events" column published a malicious attack on the People's Ticket submitted by a reader. The editor claimed it was only intended for laughs. "This came to my desk Wednesday," he noted. "It is purely political, of course, but it demonstrates the ability of someone to mix laughter with the heat and abuse of a political campaign." The letter, in part, read:

> Dear Fellow Lush:
> I am writing on behalf of THE PEOPLE'S TICKET—THE DRUNK PEOPLE'S TICKET, that is—sometimes known as the D-ticket.
> This is our platform:
>   1. Police Department:
>   A. No more roadblocks—a hazard to any drunken driver.
>   B. All drunks to be issued special license guaranteeing immunity from arrest upon proof of the consumption of 12 beers or more.
>   C. All drunks to be issued special permits authorizing bearers to insult any officer of the law.
>   . . . . . .
>   5. Government Administration:
>   A. We pledge to hold our meetings in bars in all parts of the city— these meetings will be open to anyone who can find us.[48]

Having exhausted his charges against Telles, Hooten on election eve resorted to "red-baiting" the People's Ticket:

> Does that constant hammering on "people" recall any haunting memories of other parts of the world where there are "People's Governments" and "People's Courts?" When you have nothing to sell the voters you can always set yourself up as the champion of the "people".[49]

Hooten's attacks on Telles, while in keeping with El Paso's tradition of rough political battles, could not help but hint at what in fact was the unspoken issue in the campaign: could and should a Mexican American be elected as mayor. No one had overtly made Telles's ethnic background a campaign issue as had P. D. Lowry in the 1948 county clerk race. However, no one could avoid the implications of Telles's candidacy. Mexican Americans saw in him a crusader for political representation. Many Anglos, on the other hand, worried that Telles, if elected, would favor Mexican Americans and corrupt local government. Rumors floated during the early campaign, for example, that he would make wholesale personnel changes in the police department and replace Anglos with "Chicanos." Albert Armendáriz recalls leaflets passed out in northeast El Paso, not necessarily by the Rogers campaign, suggesting that Telles as mayor would "fill the courthouse with Mexicans." One Anglo leader, according to Ted Bender, stated that the challenger would "Mexicanize" El Paso politics: "That all the evils that Mexican politics is heir to would be vested upon El Paso." To Bender, the anti-Mexican feeling in the election was clear, but hard to pin down: "You could feel it, but you couldn't grasp it. It's like a ghost." Telles recounts that some Anglo friends shied away from his candidacy undoubtedly because of the ethnic issue:

> I'd have a . . . good friend of mine, an Anglo friend of mine, we'd been friends maybe six, eight years and probably [he] supported me as County Clerk, but when I solicited his support for the Mayor's job he'd say: "Ray, (he'd say) look, you've been an

excellent County Clerk; you've done a tremendous job. I know that if you want to be reelected you can be reelected as many times as you want to; you can stay there the rest of your life, but from there it's something else."[50]

He was not bothered about such reactions, but understood why they affected the campaign:

You see what really happened was the fact that this was the first time in the history that a Mexican American had even dared [run for mayor], not only jump in the campaign, but even think about it, you know. And so many people, and this was true of Texas and probably the whole country, I don't know. But the thing about it was that many people, they couldn't see the City of El Paso being represented by a Mexican American.[51]

Some Anglos could not accept Telles as an authentic American and instead viewed him and all Mexican Americans as foreigners. One writer to the *Times*, for example, suggested that a vote for Rogers was a vote for Americanism and for security:

Happy, safe American homes are made possible by the liberties secured by the Constitution, so let us keep it American and not forget the patriots who sat at the table of liberty in the infancy of this nation.

    On this election let us keep a course of safety which leads to security, happiness and perpetuity for our City of El Paso. Your vote for our present mayor will keep it so.[52]

Telles's candidacy likewise disturbed some Anglo Protestants. Whether his Catholic religion or his ethnicity repelled them is difficult to determine. In any event, he recalls that particular Protestant ministers actively and openly supported Rogers from their pulpits. Cleofas Calleros, longtime El Paso historian and social worker, noted in his weekly column in the *Times* that the religious issue had been injected into the campaign. "Unfortunately," he wrote, "the present City political campaign suffered such 'happenings' because the 'little man and woman, the little brain, the bigoted and the prej-udiced' have seen fit to conduct an underhanded whispering cam-paign (unknown to both candidates) to bring forth the same kind of propaganda that was extensively used in the 1920s during the Ku Klux Klan terror." Calleros specifically observed in a letter of protest to Hooten, Rogers, and Judson Williams that the executive committee of the Ancient and Accepted Scottish Rite of Freema-sonry in El Paso had since January been distributing notices to their members, reminding them of the principle of separation of church and state in the United States and of the dangers of any religion attempting to impose its authority over the government. One such notice, according to Calleros, read: "Yet we find within our borders many irrefutable evidences of continuing efforts on the part of the Roman hierarchy to do just that." Calleros believed that such a warning was aimed at the Telles campaign. He labeled such tactics as "vicious and racial propaganda" which was well "timed" for the mayoral election.[53]

Calleros called for religious toleration. "It was a mean, ugly sit-uation," Richard Telles remembers of the religion issue. However, despite some bitter disputes between the Masons and the Catholic Knights of Columbus over the Telles candidacy, Calleros convinced the Catholic hierarchy to intervene with Protestant leaders to sub-due the controversy.[54]

CHAPTER FOUR

Richard Telles
and
Barrio Politics

W hile Raymond Telles conducted his public campaign in
organized political forums, in the newspapers, and on television, he approved of the "unofficial campaign" being carried out in
the streets, alleys, cantinas, community centers, and homes of the
barrio. There, Richard Telles put his organizing talents to work
and proved indispensable to his brother's campaign. "I was the
mean guy," Richard observes of his work in the campaign. "I was
the guy with the black hat. I did the dirty work." "Richard was *the
man*," Ted Bender recalls. And "Lelo" Jacques of LULAC notes
that Richard was the "Mexican Lyndon Johnson—master politician." Intensely loyal to Raymond and harboring his own political
ambitions, Richard understood that ethnicity was the name of the
game in the election. Raymond might officially present himself as a
public servant above ethnicity, but Richard mobilized the Mexican
American hunger for the election of one of their own as mayor.
They were tired of being treated as second-class citizens and hoped
that through the electoral process they could achieve political

respectability and eliminate barriers to equal opportunities. "We started feeling the pressure of social justice," Richard explains. "We wanted a little cut of the pie."[1]

Richard concentrated solely on the Mexican American neighborhoods in south and southeast El Paso in establishing his own campaign organization separate from the official Telles headquarters downtown. "We stayed away from it completely," he recalls. "We knew what we had to do, and we did it from our office in south El Paso." He ran his part of the campaign out of his own business quarters at Eighth and South St. Vrain Streets in the same house his father had built for the family. Here, veterano Navarrete explains, the "nuts and bolts" of the campaign took place. "He knew precincts," Ralph Seitsinger tells of Richard, "he knew who was there, he knew who were the workers." Only a massive Mexican American turnout would elect his brother, and Richard believed only he could organize the vote. Marantz might be the official campaign manager, but "Ritchie" Telles was the unofficial one and as he puts it: "When it came down to the strategy and all that, very few people knew how to handle south and east El Paso." He might have added that he was one of the few.[2]

As in the 1948 campaign, Richard Telles's first task consisted of registering Mexican Americans to vote. With the veteranos of the Segura McDonald VFW Post, along with additional veterans from the south-side Marcos V. Armijo VFW unit, Telles again assembled a sophisticated political organization in the best tradition of American ethnic politics. He and the veteranos overcame the discriminating poll tax by appealing everywhere for money. "The money was the number-one thing," Richard emphasizes. "We hocked our souls." To legitimize these and other campaign operations, Richard organized out of his office the Southside Democratic Club, composed primarily of veteranos who could not officially engage in politics as a VFW group. A diversity of sources contributed funds. "Kiko" Hernández recalls that many like himself gave out of their own pockets. Mexican American merchants donated. Even the mayor of Juárez, René Mascareñas, who had attended Cathedral High School with Raymond, provided financial assistance.[3]

With these funds, Richard and more than seven hundred Mexican American members of the two VFW posts, along with other volunteers, fanned throughout the barrios to register voters and assist those who could not afford the poll tax. The Telles forces, as in 1948, made use of Richard's business contacts in the cantinas and used these establishments as organizing centers. "It was the easiest way to organize," Richard says of the cantina strategy. "There wasn't a business in south El Paso that I didn't know or had something to do with." In fact, Richard himself owned several of these businesses. At the cantinas, Mexican Americans could pay their poll taxes or, if they did not have the $1.75, Telles supporters gave it to them. In addition, Richard selected district coordinators and precinct captains who supervised door-to-door contacts encouraging registration. "I knew all the people," coordinator David Villa notes, "they knew me since I was that high." The veteranos likewise held dances where Mexican Americans purchased admission by paying a poll tax. The women's auxiliaries of the VFW aided these efforts as well by selling poll tax receipts at community halls.[4]

Mexican Americans, as noted earlier, responded enthusiastically to Raymond Telles's candidacy and registered in large numbers. Richard Telles recalls that although the Rogers campaign had not taken Raymond's challenge seriously at first, they certainly did after they realized the size of the Mexican American vote being put together. "But by then, it was too late," he concludes. "We had the people well organized. We had our precinct leaders. They couldn't touch us."[5]

To publicize the campaign, Richard took advantage of border culture by purchasing time on Juárez radio stations that provided cheaper rates than in El Paso. The Spanish-language political ads easily reached across the narrow Rio Grande and into Mexican American homes. These ads, along with the campaign in general, also made Raymond Telles something of a political hero in Juárez. Moreover, Richard stored posters and bumper stickers in his headquarters for volunteers to distribute two weeks before the election. Richard, along with David Villa, also personally visited local community organizations such as PTAs in south-side schools where he called on Mexican American parents to vote for his brother and to "stand up and be counted." Besides organized activities, word-of-mouth efforts spread news of the Telles campaign. Druggist Hernández remembers talking to his customers about the election as well as displaying Telles posters in his windows.[6]

Registering voters and publicizing the campaign, Richard likewise educated Mexican Americans on the process of voting. Voter education became doubly important because city officials for the first time employed voting machines in the city election. Richard believed that the use of the machines in an election with a Mexican American candidate was no coincidence. He saw it as an attempt to intimidate potential Mexican American voters. To overcome these obstacles, Richard ingeniously devised mock voting machines out of empty refrigerator boxes. He placed these samples at every precinct before and during election day to demonstrate to the people how to operate the machines. The mock-ups resembled regular machines and volunteers instructed voters how to pull the correct lever alongside each of the People's Ticket candidates. "Don't be scared," Ray Marantz recalls instructors telling voters, "go ahead and vote. You have the privilege and the right to vote." In addition, Ted Bender remembers that some Mexican Americans received a string with knots like a rosary. Telles supporters instructed voters to take this string into the regular voting machines, hang the string alongside the names of candidates, and pull the lever where the knots corresponded to one of the People's Ticket candidates. Other voters memorized a fictitious telephone number provided by the Telles people whose figures matched the correct placement on the ballot of each candidate of the People's Ticket. Although these tactics undoubtedly disturbed the Rogers campaigners, they put up no serious challenge to them. "I don't see how they let us," "Kiko" Hernández still wonders about the mock machine placed outside Jefferson High School, "but we did it."[7]

On election day, Richard finely orchestrated his organization to deliver the vote. From command headquarters in his office, he observed on a big board the total number of registered voters in each Mexican American precinct and the actual number voting as

*Right and Below:
Facsimile of
electronic voting
booth devised by
Richard Telles,
south El Paso, 1957.
Courtesy
Raymond L. Telles*

the day progressed. He broke down a list of all registered voters and delegated his volunteers to be responsible for not only particular areas, but specific individuals. Every registered Mexican American received individual attention from a volunteer. "We had no computer or anything," Telles recalls. "We'd take those lists, take the names down, break this into streets, break them into numbers, and go from there. It was a hell of a job!"[8]

In a separate room at headquarters, David Villa operated three telephones connecting him with district coordinators and precinct captains, who would request information on which precinct a particular voter was eligible to vote in. In the field, volunteers including veteranos and LULAC members contacted people in their homes to see if they had voted. Others drove voters to the polls. As in 1948, Delfina Telles assisted her husband by encouraging friends and acquaintances to vote for him. Each volunteer reported to a precinct captain who, along with district coordinators, reported regularly to central headquarters. Still others, including young Mexican women sent over by Juárez Mayor Mascareñas to help, passed out sample ballots at each precinct. "We made sure that every man who had a poll tax went out to vote," Richard explains. "We physically picked the people up from their homes and brought them to vote." As he supervised the election turnout both from his office and in the streets, Richard grew confident that his brother had won.[9]

With the help of the veteranos, the LULAC members, and countless others, Richard Telles masterminded the most impressive Mexican American vote in the history of El Paso. Whether Raymond won or lost, Richard had displayed the political strength of Mexican Americans when organized. "I don't think that there has ever been," lawyer Armendáriz stresses, "as high a participation in any political campaign of a Mexican American community as we experienced on this day when we elected Raymond Telles."[10]

With the flurry of activity on election day, the campaign came to an end. Only the results awaited. Campaign manager Marantz believed that Telles and Rogers were even, although no scientific polls existed. In its afternoon edition, the *Herald-Post* headlined a Telles lead determined from polling voters in certain precincts.

The paper estimated that the rest of the People's Ticket held substantial margins over their opponents. El Pasoans voted in record numbers. The *Herald-Post* predicted a final vote of at least 30,000, almost double that of the 1955 city election. The polls closed at 7 p.m. and Telles, exhausted from the campaign, waited for the returns at home. As in 1948, he believed he had failed to get the vote out and had lost. Early returns from pro-Rogers precincts only darkened his mood. Telles reconciled himself to possible defeat. "But I was satisfied that we had done everything we could. If we hadn't won, at least we had opened the doors for someone else to try it next time. . . . In other words, it would be a lot easier the next time for somebody else to try it 'cause we had already opened the road or broken the ice with having a Hispanic candidate, which we hadn't had before." Precinct returns from the south side, however, soon lifted his hopes. "Then I decided well, gee whiz, maybe I better go down to the courthouse and see what's going on."[11]

At the courthouse, Telles and Rogers supporters clustered around to hear the returns from the last precinct boxes. "I knew how far behind we were, of course," Telles recalls, "'cause they were being counted—tabulated—all the time and I knew that we had certain precincts of ours which would come in pretty heavy for us, you know, and it started coming in and, sure enough, before too long after that, we pulled up side by side and then we starting pulling away." By 10 p.m., officials finished the count and announced the results. With a record city election vote of 34,883, Telles upset Rogers by 2,754 votes: 18,688 to 15,934 (53.97 percent of the vote). Moreover, the entire People's Ticket won with even larger margins. Telles supporters celebrated well into the next day. Veterano Navarrete remembers that he and other elated volunteers paraded around the courthouse and staged a brief victory march into south El Paso. For Telles, delight was mixed with sobriety:

> There was excitement, but it was inside and I was trying to
> understand what had happened, you know. Because of the odds,
> I honestly didn't think I could win, but I was going to give it a

good try. And then all of a sudden here it is: "You have won, now it is your responsibility, what are you going to do with it?" And all of a sudden . . . like a cold shower—I realized what I had gotten into.[12]

Telles won because his strategy worked. His sterling military and political record, his dignified personal appearance, and his avoidance of an ethnic public campaign disarmed all but the most racist Anglo voters. The opposition could not isolate him as a threat to the city's interests or portray him as a radical Mexican American. Consequently, Telles gained a certain percentage of Anglo votes while conceding to Rogers only a minute fraction of Mexican American ones. With Pooley's help, Telles instead placed Rogers on the defensive by exploiting issues such as the Lower Valley annexation. At the same time, Telles remained calm when his opponents counterattacked. Moreover, through the work of Richard Telles, the veteranos, and the LULACs, Telles effectively mobilized Mexican American voters. "That was a revolution, not an election," one Mexican American exclaimed.[13]

To win, Telles needed landslide margins in south and southeast El Paso. He had to win or do very well in precincts just north of the tracks that were mixed but becoming predominantly Mexican American. He also had to win with solid margins in the Lower Valley. Finally, he had to pick up enough Anglo voters throughout the city to deprive Rogers of comparable victories in Anglo precincts. The Telles campaign accomplished all these goals. In south and southeast El Paso, he achieved his landslide: 5,211 to Rogers's 602. Telles won almost 90 percent of the vote (89.6) in these precincts, exactly the percentage he had figured would be needed to win office. His supporters turned out 82.5 percent of registered voters in these 10 precincts. In the Lower Valley, he won all nine precincts by 5,498 to 2,768, or 66.5 percent of the vote. The Lower Valley, according to Ralph Seitsinger, proved to be the swing vote. Together, south and southeast El Paso along with the Lower Valley provided Telles with 10,709 votes out of his total of 18,688, or 57 percent of his total. He combined this support with good success in northern precincts containing growing numbers of Mexican Americans. In the Upper Valley he won Precinct 4, Smeltertown, where the Mexican American local of the Mine, Mill, and Smelter Union workers delivered 288 voters for Telles to Rogers's 29. In west El Paso, he won Precincts 7 and 8 in the Sunset Heights district. In the lower portions of northeast El Paso, he took three precincts, and in the northwest (including the central downtown district with significant numbers of Mexican Americans), he led six out of eight precincts with 1,517 to Rogers's 1,401, or 51.8 percent of the vote. In all, Telles won 31 out of 53 precincts. Additionally, he cut into Anglo precincts and denied his opponent landslide victories of his own by winning 30.3 percent of the totals in those northern precincts won by Rogers (4,609 to Rogers's 10,595). Albert Armendáriz believes this Anglo percentage for Telles represented liberal Democrats.[14]

Rogers's loss did not lie in his inability to turn out Anglo voters. He amassed as high a percentage of Anglo voters as did Telles among Mexican Americans. In Rogers's strongholds of northeast El Paso and the exclusive Kern Place, he won 16 out of 19 precincts and drew 80.7 percent of the voters. In the end, however, Rogers failed to match the large Mexican American vote both on the south side and in those mixed northern precincts, along with the Lower Valley. The *Times* conceded that these areas gave Telles a "runaway lead" that Rogers could not overcome. The victory, of course, was sweetened by the election of the entire People's Ticket. Underscoring Telles's more controversial candidacy, all of his aldermen, who were required to run city-wide races, were chosen by substantial margins. Craigo won by 5,777, Bender by 5,268, Seitsinger by 7,989, and White by 7,625 votes.[15]

Telles, relieved and grateful, acknowledged his victory in the Democratic primary and looked forward to being officially elected in the normally uncontested general election. "I am grateful to the people who supported me," he stated. "I'm proud of the way the people of El Paso went out and voted. We want the people to control the reins of government and as long as they vote, we have nothing to fear from any source." His only regret was that his father and his mother were not alive to see their son elected mayor of El Paso. An equally ecstatic Pooley congratulated the victors and in true Rooseveltian tradition proclaimed a "New Deal" at City Hall: "Mayor Raymond Telles is not under obligation to any person or group. He and his aldermen ran on their merits. They are good, patriotic citizens, seeking nothing but an opportunity to serve the people. They carried 30 [31] of the City's 53 precincts. There isn't any questions about it: they are the people's choice." On the other side, Rogers expressed pleasure at the record turnout of voters, thanked the people for supporting him during his tenure as mayor, and extended his best wishes to the new administration.[16]

Not all El Pasoans, however, proved as gracious as the incumbent in defeat. Hooten and the *Times*, for example, congratulated Telles, but planted doubts about his votes. Hooten complained that too much flexibility had been allowed in the sale of poll taxes. He specifically objected to the number of private individuals who sold them. Instead, Hooten believed "the place to pay a poll tax is at the Court House or at other designated places over which regular deputies of the tax collectors preside." Moreover, he publicized three "glaring situations" that had been brought to his attention concerning poll tax irregularities. One man reported that he possessed two poll tax receipts. He had bought one and had been given another by a "friend." In a second case, a man living across the border in Juárez claimed to have obtained a poll tax by giving an El Paso address. Finally, Hooten alleged that a south El Paso woman had phoned him and reported being allowed to vote at Aoy School even though her name was not on the voting list, but she had a poll tax receipt. "I'm not saying that there was any intentional violation of the law," Hooten proposed. "Those things were either through ignorance of the law or occurred during the excitement. But I do say that the system ought to be changed." Still, Hooten's charges of irregularities—despite no formal complaints or indictments during or after the campaign—indicated a reluctance to accept the Telles victory and indirectly encouraged a movement to deny him the mayor's office in the general election scheduled for 9 April.[17]

Victory in the Democratic primary was tantamount to election in El Paso as well as elsewhere in Texas. Few registered Republicans functioned at the local level. Consequently, Telles believed that the general election as in past years would simply be pro forma and he and his ticket would be unopposed. But Telles was no ordinary candidate. He was a Mexican American. The first hint of possible opposition came shortly after the primary when outgoing Mayor Rogers consolidated the city's 53 precincts into 16 for the general election. Rogers argued that this would save $4,500 in election costs. The Telles campaign, however, feared that reducing precincts would lower the number of voters by making it difficult to get to the polls. This would be especially true in the barrios where many lacked transportation. The reduction of voters, particularly Mexican Americans, might leave Telles vulnerable to a write-in challenge. Hooten at the *Times* scoffed at such fears and noted that no opposition to Telles had appeared. Instead, he accused the People's Ticket of wanting to squander money away on the general election. Perhaps, Hooten suggested, this was an omen of Telles's future budgeting policies. The *Times* editor went further and proposed discarding altogether the primary system in local elections. "We do not need that expensive bit of politics," he concluded. "All we need is a direct election denied of partisanship, with a runoff a week later if needed to establish a majority winner." Hooten conveniently failed to note that removing the primary would increase the role of "closet" Republicans like himself and make it easier for them to more comfortably run for local office without being tied in any way to the Democratic party. The editor, of course, had not voiced doubts about the primary until this election.[18]

Opposition to the consolidation quickly surfaced. Pooley called it illegal and advised Mayor Rogers to consult with city attorneys. "Then," Pooley added, "we hope he will order the unlawful action brushed aside and give back to the people the convenience of their own precincts." Former county attorney Ernest Guinn observed that no provision in the Texas election laws existed for such consolidation. Confident of their legal position, the Telles ticket formally protested Rogers's actions. Ted Bender and Ernie Craigo requested that all 53 precincts be used for the general election. If not, this would disenfranchise voters as well as violate the law. The People's Ticket wished to avoid entering office on the basis of an illegal election that might invalidate not only the results but also their actions in office. Under pressure, Rogers announced that all 53 precincts would be activated. Pooley congratulated him for returning to the letter of the law, but still suspected other possible moves to deny Telles office. "[W]e suggest to those El Pasoans who voted and elected the People's Ticket that they be sure to vote on April 9th," he stressed. "It could be that the soreheads are planning a write-in."[19]

Rumors of a write-in campaign increased as the general election approached. The feasibility of the proposal advanced when a county official stipulated that paper ballots would be used for the general election rather than voting machines. The machines (owned by the county but lent to the city) would not be available because of their use in the U.S. Senate election one week earlier. Voters could more easily write in a candidate on paper ballots than on a machine. *El Continental* bluntly interpreted such measures as anti-Mexican moves that, along with the unsuccessful precinct consolidation, aimed to deprive Telles of office. The opposition also hoped that the challenger's forces would be spent and complacent after their primary victory. The Mexican American newspaper called on the Telles campaign to reinvigorate itself and get the vote out for the general election.[20]

Most prominently mentioned for a write-in challenge was, of course, Mayor Rogers. However, three days before the election, Rogers squelched rumors by stating that though asked to consent to a write-in, he disassociated himself from such efforts. According to Telles, Rogers told the Kingmakers: "I'm not going to do it. Ray beat me fair and square. I'm not going to do it. I've got news for you, I'm going to vote for him." Pooley commended the mayor for his conduct, but warned again: "Still the soreheads plot. They lack the sportsmanship of a rattlesnake. They make no sound. They order their stooges to find more stooges. They instruct them in how to defeat the people's will."[21]

The editor was not disappointed. Just two days before the election, M. R. Hollenshead, an unsuccessful independent candidate for alderman in the primary, agreed to a write-in campaign on his behalf. A former deputy superintendent of El Paso Public Schools, Hollenshead owned a sash and door company plus an insurance agency. The *Times* noted that thirty young business and professional men, who declined to publicly identify themselves citing fears of economic reprisals, along with several women's organizations, had initiated the write-in. They claimed several hundred volunteers and said that a large-scale telephone and mail drive would be conducted. Only Telles, and not his aldermen, would be challenged.[22]

The write-in forces opposed Telles on several grounds. They believed that many voters did not really support him, but had voted for him as a protest against the Rogers administration. They cited the Lower Valley as an example of protest voting. These voters would turn against Telles if given a "good non-political" candidate such as Hollenshead, they reasoned. Moreover, seven thousand who were eligible had failed to go to the polls in the primary and obviously disapproved of Telles. Such voters deserved another candidate. "A majority of El Paso voters did not endorse Telles," they argued, "and we do not believe that a majority is for him." They charged that Telles would establish machine politics in El Paso and called attention to his campaign: "We want to show the people that the bloc vote so effectively machine-manufactured in the last city primary for Telles can be overcome by public indignation." Furthermore, they complained that they were being cheated out of an independent mayor because of Telles's ties to Pooley. Instead, El Pasoans needed to elect "a candidate who has no private political ax to grind, no obligations or affiliations, and no entangling alliances of any kind and whose qualifications are unquestioned." Finally, the write-in campaign hinted that Telles as a Mexican American would not represent all El Pasoans. "Remember," a political ad for Hollenshead read, "You MUST scratch the name of Raymond Telles and WRITE IN the name of M. R. Hollenshead on the paper ballot that will be given to all voters."[23]

The *Times* secretly hoped for a Hollenshead upset but disguised this by appearing to be disinterested or ambivalent. Hooten claimed that his newspaper had nothing to do with the write-in but endorsed the right of Hollenshead supporters to conduct it. The editor acknowledged that he had never seen a write-in campaign succeed but at the same time stressed that a primary victory meant little. "To say that it [the primary] is the 'will of the people' to 'elect' any candidate in a primary is a misnomer," Hooten wrote. "All that a primary can do is to say that it is the will of those who participated in that primary to 'nominate' this or that candidate who will represent that party in the general election." Hooten concluded that perhaps the people had made a mistake in the primary and that the write-in would allow them to rectify it.[24]

Taking the Hollenshead write-in seriously, Telles expressed displeasure at the open effort to deprive him of his primary victory. No other mayoral candidate had ever been challenged outside the primary. "I wasn't exactly happy about it," he recalls. "I couldn't help but believe . . . they were doing it because they didn't want me in there." His forces responded by going on the attack, mobilizing their own supporters. Pooley as usual led the verbal assault by labeling Hollenshead a "sucker" for allowing the "soreheads" to use his name. He accused the candidate of not being able to take his primary defeat "like a man" and for being a traitor to the Democratic party by not supporting its nominee for mayor. Moreover, his supporters were nothing but a cowardly "yellow gang" that lacked the courage to publicly endorse Hollenshead. "Who are the organizing group?" Pooley asked. "Who is the spokesman?"[25]

Pooley also noted that Hollenshead some years earlier, while a school administrator, had intimidated teachers to vote for a particular candidate in a school board election. "It was the dirtiest election in El Paso's history," Pooley commented. "It was as un-American as the hammer and sickle." He conceded that he would not necessarily have objected to a write-in campaign organized earlier and openly. "But this 11th hour thing is indecent." The editor concluded by addressing the unspoken issue of the campaign. He accused the Hollenshead write-in of being racist and anti-Mexican.

"They are waging an un-American campaign of bigotry and prejudice. They are hurting and dividing its people." Pooley called on El Pasoans to reject this type of politics: "Vote American! Vote Telles!"[26]

El Continental seconded Pooley's charge of racism by noting that only Telles faced a write-in challenge, not his Anglo aldermanic candidates. "The only conclusion that can be reached," it editorialized "is that this campaign is discriminatory, anti-Latin, and—why not say it—anti-Catholic." Cleofas Calleros, writing to the *Herald-Post*, added that Hollenshead as a past school administrator had been associated with officials who had discriminated against Mexicans and who were now supporting the write-in:

> History repeats itself! We might as well bring it out in the open—the last minute announcement that a write-in candidate, endorsed by the same men, who in the '20s and '30s refused to have Spanish taught in the schools, should be no news. He is merely showing his color.[27]

Besides criticizing the write-in, the Telles camp once again mobilized. "We reorganized the whole campaign stronger than before," Richard Telles remembers. "We were now fighting mad." Exhausted of money from the primary, the Telles people relied on personal contact, especially in the barrios, to bring out the vote. They distributed leaflets, telephoned, and went door-to-door. On election day, Richard utilized again the same strategy of precinct captains, a transportation network, and poll watchers. "If we lose, we can never forgive ourselves," Mario Acevedo, a Telles supporter, warned.[28]

Mexican Americans heeded this advice and once again rallied to Telles's cause. They would not be denied their victory. He received almost unanimous support in the Mexican American precincts and duplicated his primary success, even carrying seven precincts earlier won by Rogers. A record 26,345 voters went to the polls in this unprecedented contested general election. In the 1955 general election only 1,118 votes had been cast. More El Pasoans cast ballots in two hours in 1957 than had voted in the entire 1955 election. Telles received 17,080 votes to Hollenshead's 8,961 and carried 38 of 53 precincts. South and southeast El Paso almost matched their total primary votes for Telles. His tally of 5,178 to Hollenshead's 205 was close to 400 votes fewer than Rogers had. Telles increased his percentage in these precincts by obtaining 96.19 percent of the total votes cast. In Precinct 12, Bowie High School, he completely shut out Hollenshead 373 to 0. In the Lower Valley, considered vulnerable to the write-in, Telles won by an even larger percentage than in the primary. He gathered 4,528 votes to Hollenshead's 1,410, or 76.25 percent of the total. Of the seven new precincts Telles won, two were in west El Paso, four in the northeast, and one in the northwest. He won in these precincts by apparently picking up more Anglo voters. Moreover, in the 15 precincts that went for Hollenshead, Telles received 36.44 percent of the total vote, up over six percentage points from the primary. In all, the victor took a substantial 65.58 percent of the total votes cast, a significant increase from his 53.97 percent in the primary. "It can be said," *El Continental* concluded, "that Telles's triumph this time was more solid than in the primary and, what is more, it was not totally determined by voters from the Mexican barrios, but from both sections of the city."[29]

A relieved but happy Telles, for the second time in a month, thanked his supporters and called for unity among all El Pasoans. He had won the election, but still close to 9,000 had voted for a minor write-in candidate. "I know there have been groups opposed to my election," he stated, "but I respect their rights and opinions and I bear no malice." His opponents accepted the general election. They could do no less. However, resentments still lingered. Hooten, for example, sarcastically wondered how Telles could possibly win every vote cast at Bowie High School. And he reminded readers of Telles's "inexperience" that would necessitate business support in order to govern effectively. "Although the *Times* opposed the People's Ticket," Hooten noted, "this newspaper most certainly will not throw any obstacles or 'roadblocks' in his path." Over at the *Herald-Post*, Pooley celebrated Telles's election by getting in one final assault on Hooten, the Kingmakers, and the anti-Telles campaign. "Let us hope those who opposed them [the People's Ticket] especially the anonymous gang of sore-heads who led the write-in campaign against Mr. Telles will be patriotic enough to help instead of hinder the new administration." And in a final assessment, Pooley urged his audience to understand that the main opposition to Telles resulted from racial prejudice. If that could be understood, then perhaps this election would have larger implications.

> Their [anti-Telles campaign] was based in prejudice and big-otry. They should have learned that such campaigns rarely win. We hope they have, and we hope they will join other El Pasoans in the effort to keep our City growing more and more prosper-ous. In that way, they will atone for the un-American fight they waged.[30]

On 11 April Raymond L. Telles officially became the first Mexican American mayor of El Paso. *El Continental* appreciated the historic moment and headlined: "Telles, Alcalde Paisano"— "Telles, 'Our' Mayor."[31]

Telles being sworn in as mayor of El Paso by
Federal Judge R. E. Thomason, 11 April 1957.
Courtesy El Paso Times

Mayor Telles

Reelected in 1959, Raymond Telles served four years as mayor of El Paso. In those two terms, his administration continued the spirit under which it was elected. That is, he symbolized the Mexican American quest for political status and recognition. This quest crossed class boundaries among the group, but clearly was pronounced among the more upwardly mobile and aspiring. Those who led the Telles victory saw in it an opportunity to assert their American citizenship and to hopefully be accepted into the mainstream. However, Mexican American electoral politics, by possessing moderate goals, contained the seeds of its own limitations and, indeed, ultimate frustration for a succeeding generation. Those who believed in the "politics of status" did not interpret electoral politics as one way of fundamentally transforming El Paso's historic class-racial system that relegated most Mexicans to exploitative working-class status. Rather, Mexican American leaders idealistically believed that electoral politics, without more

Mr. Mayor, Raymond L. Telles, circa late 1950s.
Courtesy Raymond L. Telles

intense community struggles, could open the doors to equal opportunity and translate "political equality" into economic and social
equality. This election widened the culture of opposition that Mexican Americans in El Paso had created over the years to advance
their struggle for justice and equal opportunities, but it did not
directly jeopardize the city's class-racial system and inaugurate
economic democracy.

Pursuing the "politics of status" rather than what might be termed the "politics of reconstruction," the Telles administration is perhaps better known for the political recognition and rising expectations it provided Mexican Americans than for substantive socioeconomic changes. By definition, the search for status involved acceptability by Anglos and hence discouraged more challenging ethnic politics. Telles stressed that he was mayor of all El Pasoans and shied away from appearing to favor Mexican Americans. Nonetheless, that group, after yearning to elect one of their own as mayor and only beginning to explore electoral ethnic politics, expressed pride in the new administration and exerted no extraordinary pressures on the mayor. "[W]hen he went into the south side I found him being treated very warmly, with a great deal of respect, with a great deal of admiration," *Herald-Post* reporter Ken Flynn comments on Telles's relationship with Mexican Americans. "I think that Raymond achieved something that everyone in the Mexican American community was proud of, and I think that most of the people that I talked to . . . kind of treated him as a hero." Telles pursued a moderately successful reform program that for the time satisfied most Mexican Americans. Above all, they identified with him. His success was their success. He made them believe in themselves and in their own capacities and those of their children to "make it" in America. As Richard Telles assessed his brother's election and administration: "The people knew that we could do it. We were part of the establishment."[1]

If Telles's personal success as mayor can be explained at one level by the continued support he received from Mexican Americans, it can also be understood by the reaction of El Paso's Anglo elite. The Kingmakers quickly perceived his moderate objectives and administrative capabilities; hence, rather than remaining opposed to him, they shifted to cooperating with the new administration. They came to understand that Telles posed no threat to their interests and that he needed their support to run the city. Peter Eisinger, in his study of the election of black mayors in Detroit and Atlanta in the early 1970s, observes that the politically displaced white elites faced five possible responses to black political

rule: cooperation, maintenance, subversion, contestation, and with-
drawal. In both cities, white elites favored, as in El Paso, cooperation. Eisinger identifies several reasons for this cooperative
response including the stakes that white elites had in these cities,
the dependence of the new political elites on cooperation from the
old elites, and, most importantly, the limits within the United
States on the use of politics for fundamental socioeconomic
change. "Electoral victory does not in the American context,"
Irwin Garfinkel stresses in his introduction to Eisinger's study, "set
the stage for radical transformation, but rather gradual changes."
As in Detroit and Atlanta, El Paso's Anglo elite did not withdraw
in discouragement from city affairs after Telles's victory. They
knew that his triumph meant only that Mexican Americans would
have to be dealt with more seriously in running the city and in distributing municipal resources. This the Kingmakers could accept
and adapt to what Eisinger terms the "culture of accommodation."
Indeed, this adjustment had been already evolving prior to 1957.
In this arrangement, the Kingmakers retained their dominant
class position as bankers and big businessmen. As Eisinger further
notes, no internal mechanism exists in American government
that could threaten the material interests of the dominant class
since the hegemonic political culture is geared to protecting their
interests:

> Political defeat [for white elites] is not life-threatening, nor
> does it result in dispossession, exile, discriminatory or confiscat-
> ing taxation, or the withdrawal of civil liberties. Neither is the
> maintenance of privileged class status profoundly linked to con-
> trol of political office, for the notion of expropriation is anath-
> ema to American political practice. In short, survival—and the
> survival of privilege—does not hinge on political victory. Losers
> in American politics can therefore live with their loss and sur-
> vive in the new order virtually as well as they lived in the old.
> This does not mean that political office is unimportant at some
> level, but that the scope of American politics must be looked at
> in its proper perspective.[2]

Mayor Telles and family, circa late 1950s.
Wife, Delfina, and daughters, Cynthia, left, and Patricia, right.,
Courtesy El Paso Times

Within this context, Telles proved to be a moderately reformist mayor. His proudest reform was to do away with convict labor through the use of chain gangs. Other reforms included better facilities for prisoners in city jail, increased flood control projects, extension of city services to the recently annexed Lower Valley, a more socially responsible police force, the condemnation of certain slum tenements in south El Paso, and the extension of urban renewal including low-cost housing in that area, street and sidewalk improvements in low-income neighborhoods, additional parks and recreation centers in different parts of the city, and airport modernization. Moreover, his administration remained relatively open and responsive to the public. He conducted, especially during his first two-year term, neighborhood meetings. As he had done as county clerk, Mayor Telles kept his office accessible to citizens. On more than one occasion, he and the city council changed their policies after hearing from particular neighborhood organizations. "It is certainly nice," the Skyline Civic and Improvement Association wrote to the *Herald-Post*, "that the Administration as such, the mayor, the Council, and the Planning Commission, stands ready to listen in a spirit of helpfulness to people who find themselves in a rather hopeless situation, if the doors of the City Hall are closed to them."[3]

As part of his reform program, Telles in a quiet fashion successfully hired more qualified Mexican Americans to city jobs. A few had served as policemen, but he accelerated their appointments as officers. In the fire department almost no Mexican Americans could be found until the Telles years. In addition, increased numbers of Mexican Americans obtained clerical positions along with their traditional roles as city laborers. Telles further appointed more of them to nonpaying city commissions. He insisted, however, that they not be given jobs simply because of their ethnicity. They had to be qualified. Telles believed that he provided Mexican Americans with the opportunities to show that they could perform as well as Anglos. "[W]e didn't favor anyone because of his name or because of his background or anything," he recalls. "We did open doors to all of those who were qualified and that in itself was an accomplishment."[4]

Lawyer Albert Armendáriz remembers Telles's concern about discrimination in city jobs when he took office. The new mayor believed he could not openly attack this process without jeopardizing his administration. Instead, he appointed men such as Alfonso Kennard and Armendáriz to the civil service commission and asked them to investigate the matter and institute changes. Armendáriz quickly discovered that both the police and fire departments refused to accept qualified Mexican Americans and that the commission sanctioned such discrimination. Only a handful of them in either department had been approved and only under exceptional circumstances. When asked by Armendáriz why almost no Mexican Americans served in the fire department,

Mayor Telles in south El Paso, circa late 1950s.
Courtesy Raymond L. Telles

the fire chief responded that his men slept all in one room and "how could we expect white boys to sleep with Mexicans?" Armendáriz's investigation and revelations forced the commission to adopt new hiring procedures that led to the appointment of Mexican American policemen and firemen. Armendáriz notes that Telles never claimed credit for this breakthrough. It was not in his nature to boast of such things. Nevertheless, his quiet leadership integrated city departments. "That's the reason that we have a Mexican American Chief of Police today," Armendáriz concluded in 1982. "This is a product of Raymond Telles."[5]

The mayor was also not afraid to tackle discrimination in public facilities. Discrimination here did not involve Mexican Americans, but it did affect African Americans who constituted no more than 2 percent of the city's population. At the Plaza Theater, El Paso's showcase movie house, African Americans could purchase tickets but had to sit in the back rows of the balcony. This was not acceptable to Telles. As mayor, he met with the Plaza's management. He recalls that in a diplomatic but forceful manner, he informed them that if they did not abandon their discriminatory policy, they would face legal action by the city. "The procedure of discrimination against blacks," Telles notes, "was immediately stopped."[6]

Telles administered a financially solvent city government. A prudent individual by nature, he regularly balanced the municipal budget while providing more services to an expanding population, but without increasing taxes. "He has an understanding of detail reports," the *Herald-Post* assessed his first six months in office. "He watches the pennies, scrutinizes requests carefully, and insists that department heads sell him, point by point, on new and unusual requests. He is not afraid to say no." In his second year in office, Telles successfully sponsored a $9.2-million bond issue that was approved by the voters for various city services. The conservative *Times* gave him high marks for his handling of the city's finances. "If the *Times* had any criticism to make of the Telles administration's new budget," Hooten wrote in 1959, "it would be that it is too small."[7]

Despite national economic recession during the late 1950s, the Telles administration was aided by an expanding border economy based on increased military expenditures for nearby Fort Bliss and White Sands Missile Range, a growing garment industry attracted to the border by cheap labor, increasing retail outlets serving a wide regional population including northern Mexico, and a booming home construction industry supported by the city's population growth from 130,485 in 1950 to close to 300,000 by 1960 (over 50 percent Spanish surnamed). Telles further gained the confidence of the business community by promoting the recruitment of new industries. In 1959 he established the El Paso Industrial Committee composed of key bankers and businessmen—Pooley's Kingmakers—to help study plans for attracting new industries. As part of his pro-business efforts, he approved the proposal by downtown businessmen to route the new east-west freeway through the center of the city. He acknowledges that after his election many Anglo businessmen feared he might retaliate against them. "But it was not my intention at all," he emphasizes,

> my intention was to run a good city, period, and I and the Council worked at it. I knew many . . . large businesses when they had business with the city, they would approach me with their tail between their legs. . . . They didn't know what was going to be our reaction. But once they were convinced that we were not going to take the action or any vengeance . . . why then everything went off pretty smooth.[8]

Efficient and businesslike, the administration was likewise noted for its honesty. Only one minor scandal scarred the record, and that occurred late in the second term. City personnel director Thomas Casso, a Telles appointee, provided advance copies of a civil service exam to two undercover detectives. After an investigation, Telles dismissed several employees implicated in the cheating and obtained the firing of Casso by the civil service commission. Although controversial, the incident did not taint Telles's own integrity.[9]

As the first Mexican American mayor of El Paso, Telles had certain advantages in pursuing his own form of border policy with neighboring Ciudad Juárez. Part of this advantage in bettering cooperation with the Mexican border city involved his close personal relationship with René Mascareñas, the mayor of Juárez at that time and his former schoolmate at Cathedral High School. Telles's close association with Juárez plus his status as mayor led to his being invited, along with Delfina, to attend as honored guests the inauguration of Adolfo López Mateos as president of Mexico in 1958.[10]

Telles worked hard to be a good mayor and his success in large part resulted from long hours of labor. "He works 12 hours practically every day," one reporter observed. "He often works 14 or 16 hours. He usually is at his desk before 8 a.m., works all day, goes home to a quiet dinner with his family, then often returns to City

Mayor Telles and duties of office, circa late 1950s.
Courtesy Raymond L. Telles

Hall for a solitary night session. Most of the time, he is the last man to leave City Hall at night." Fulfilling his promise to be a "People's Mayor," he regularly attended community and club meetings and listened to issues and complaints. "In El Paso, the people want to see [the mayor]," he explained in 1959. "It's not me personally they want to see, but the City official." Spending many evenings away from home, he was dubbed by his children "Mr. Meeting."[11]

The question of whether Telles might have done more as mayor, especially as the first Mexican American one, is a debatable issue. His supporters insist that he probably was the best mayor El Paso had had for some time. Others, including some Mexican Americans today, believe that he was too cautious and unwilling to offend Anglos, especially businessmen, by moving for greater improvements in the barrios. "He could have done a lot more," one former supporter assessed the Telles years. In the case of slum eradication, for example, he did not push for a city code that would have penalized absentee tenement owners for their lack of improvements. Even Pooley at the *Herald-Post*, during Telles's second term, accused the mayor of being too deliberate in handling increased juvenile delinquency and in dismissing incompetent officials.[12]

Telles might have gone further on specific Mexican American problems if one assumes that he was prepared to chance racial-ethnic polarization in the city. However, he was neither a gambler nor a social crusader. Conservative in personal and social outlook, he was in retrospect a moderate reformer, but one more liberal for his own historical period. "His careful and cautious approach," a reporter noted, "has surprised those of his opponents who feared he might come into City Hall with a broom, making a clean sweep and appointing his friends to office." The *Herald-Post* called Telles an "instinctive middle-of-the-roader." As mayor, he did not interpret his role as an advocate for social causes. He believed, as did many of his Mexican American contemporaries, that justice was possible through established institutions rather than through direct action in the streets. "As is often the case," D'Antonio and Form conclude in their study of "influentials" in El Paso, "minority groups may outdo Anglo-Americans in living up to the ideal beliefs and sentiments of the society."[13] Indeed, Telles viewed the running of city government, as did the Kingmakers, as a business operation. "He looks more like a serious-minded junior executive than like the traditional cartoon version of the fat, jovial, cigar-smoking politician," a reporter described him.

Even if Telles had proved more "radical," certain constraints existed that both politically and structurally would have made it difficult—although perhaps not impossible—to achieve greater reforms. For one, the Anglo establishment closely monitored him. It undoubtedly exerted indirect pressure to prevent him from instituting too populist measures that it felt might endanger the privileged status of the Kingmakers based on access and relationship to Mexican Americans as a source of cheap labor power. Telles, as mentioned, believed that as the first Mexican American

Mayor Telles revisiting St. Mary's School, circa late 1950s.
Courtesy Raymond L. Telles

mayor his first duty to himself and the people who had elected him
was to prove beyond any doubt that he could capably administer
city hall. In this he succeeded and perhaps his major accomplishment was in proving that a Mexican American, rather than plung-
ing the community into economic chaos, as his opponents had

warned, instead would help create a relatively prosperous city. Joe Herrera, city clerk under the Telles administration, recalls the skeptical scrutiny under which the mayor worked: "The general public, they just didn't know what to expect of a Latin being the mayor of this community as to whether he was just going to tear things up, or a lot of them would look to him as if we were going to become like a 'presidente municipal' [mayor] of Ciudad Juárez ... 'la mordida' [bribes] and all that sort of stuff.... I even had people ask me: 'Is he going to take any bribes'. ... People were just expecting him to go down the drain at the beginning."[14]

Only in a quiet way, did Telles believe he could advance reforms that would aid Mexican Americans. To do more, in his mind, would risk concerted opposition to his reelection bid and lead to possible defeat. Second, even had Telles decided to challenge the establishment, it is questionable how much he could have accomplished through the limited resources of city government to create anything even resembling a social revolution. Not even more "progressive" black or Mexican American mayors in recent years have been able to do this. As Eisinger explains: "City governments can do very little on their own of a systematic nature to create large numbers of jobs, redistribute income, or provide great amounts of good housing."

> Even assuming the existence of the requisite social technology, it is clear that the limits of politics in America mean that city governments—as indeed any level of government—probably cannot fashion thorough, successful, and speedy policies to deal with the big social justice problems of poverty, discrimination, unemployment, housing, or the quality of urban life.[15]

What local governments at least can do, Eisinger suggests, is to address such problems in an incremental and piecemeal fashion. Hence, incrementalism might best characterize the Telles approach to the relationship between city government and social reform. He believed that Mexican Americans would advance not so much by what government could do for them, but by increased educational opportunities and by the introduction of new businesses and industries that would create more and better jobs. Unfortunately, Telles, tied to administering a city dependent on Mexican labor, failed to appreciate the contradictions between his belief in the remunerative powers of private enterprise and the drive by private enterprise, especially along the border, to secure the cheapest labor possible from the minority community.

If the Telles years did not produce extraordinary social reforms, his administration nevertheless was a political success story. From a Mexican American candidate engaged in one of El Paso's most heated and controversial elections, he in four years became the "darling" of El Paso politics. He accomplished this by, on the one hand, maintaining overwhelming Mexican American support and, on the other, by astutely building ties to the Anglo establishment. In the 1959 city election no one dared to challenge him. His aldermen faced token opposition and won reelection by wide margins. His political influence as well as his "acceptability" by the establishment was marked in February 1959 when the El Paso Ministerial Association, some of whose members had questioned Telles's Catholicism two years earlier, endorsed his performance as mayor. They did not openly admit it, but the churchmen essentially praised Telles for not dividing the city along ethnic lines. "We are aware," the association observed,

> that our community could have fallen into a divisive competition with various groups pursuing their special interest with little regard for the welfare of the entire community. We are also aware that you have made every effort to deal with each issue in the best interest of the whole community and so have set a high standard and pattern by which every group in our community could measure itself.[16]

The *El Paso Times* did not publicly endorse Telles for reelection, but raised no opposition. "Ordinarily," Hooten wrote, "The *Times* believes in a second term, under the Democratic way of doing things." Pooley at the *Herald-Post* considered Telles's uncontested reelection proof that a Mexican American could be a good mayor. "Let us hope," he stressed, "that the lack of opposition to Mayor

Mayor Telles with Ciudad Juárez Mayor René Mascareñas
at U.S.-Mexico border, August 1959.
Courtesy Raymond L. Telles

Telles means the end of hyphenated Americanism in El Paso. Any American, regardless of ancestry, is eligible to be the mayor of their city, be he Latin-American or Nordic-American."[17]

Telles, of course, did not escape some political tensions during his two terms. He feuded with County Judge Woodrow Bean over proper city-county jurisdiction. His alderman in charge of police affairs, Jack White, became embarrassingly controversial and a political irritant. And Pooley increasingly criticized Telles's cautious manner.

The mayor's successful support for abolishing the Democratic primary in city elections went against the wishes of some Democratic party leaders as well as those of Ed Pooley. The argument for the elimination of the party primary system, which in El Paso only involved Democrats since the Republican party was almost

*Mayor Telles attending the inauguration of Adolfo López Mateos
as president of Mexico, 5 December 1958.
Toasting outgoing President Adolfo Ruiz Cortines, left.
In center is Federico Mariscal, director of protocol
of the Mexican government.*
Courtesy El Paso Times

nonexistent then, was that it made no financial sense to have a primary followed by a general election since traditionally victory in the Democratic primary was tantamount to election. Having two elections within a few weeks of each other cost too much money, argued proponents of eliminating the primary.

Mayor Telles agreed. In addition, he favored dropping the primary because of his own experience in the 1957 election when the dual election process had been used to try to deny him his smashing primary victory. As far as Telles was concerned, one election—a nonpartisan city election—was sufficient. The opponents of the antiprimary movement, led by Pooley and the *Herald-Post*, countered that elimination of the party primary would weaken Democratic party allegiance and make it easier for "closet" Republicans to run for office without disclosing their party affiliation.

In the 1959 city elections, voters were asked to approve or disapprove a change in the city charter on retaining a party primary. With very little opposition, the proposal to eliminate the primary was approved and went into effect in the 1961 local elections. It has been suggested that the erasure of the Democratic primary in El Paso's city elections and its replacement by a nonpartisan one after 1961 affected, perhaps negatively, Mexican American electoral participation. Yet there is little evidence to support this. Since 1961 the number of Mexican American candidates in city elections has substantially increased as well as the number elected to the city council.

Although Telles had found himself on opposite sides of the primary issue with some of his supporters including Pooley, this was not enough to cause any long-term friction. Indeed, Telles's nonpartisan stand on the party primary only served to increase his stature with El Pasoans. They increasingly saw him as someone who stood above politics. His dignified and gentlemanly style disarmed even his critics and gave him the aura of a statesman rather than a politician. Telles, himself, believes that perhaps his most important accomplishment was to bring unity to the city after a divisive period including the 1957 election. In 1961, his choice was not whether he could win a third term—most conceded that he could—but whether he still wanted to be mayor.[18]

*Mayor Telles with
County Judge
Woodrow Bean,
circa late 1950s.
Courtesy* El Paso
Times

*Mayor Telles presenting keys of
the city to Sen. Lyndon B.
Johnson, 31 August 1959.
Courtesy* El Paso Herald-Post

The year 1961 proved to be a major political watershed for
Raymond Telles and for Mexican American politics in El Paso. He
faced two political alternatives. He could run for reelection or seek
an appointment in John Kennedy's New Frontier. He had supported the Massachusetts senator after Kennedy won the Democratic nomination and had campaigned in California among Mexican
Americans for the Kennedy-Johnson ticket. In California, he campaigned with Sen. Dennis Chávez of New Mexico. They traveled
from San Francisco to San Diego speaking for Kennedy. In El
Paso, both Telles and Chávez hosted a pro-Kennedy rally. Political
pundits believed the new president would offer Telles a position in
the new administration as a response to the strong Mexican American vote he had received. Rumors flew shortly after the election
that Telles might even be appointed ambassador to Mexico.[19]

Telles, however, announced for reelection in early January
1961. He knew that it would be weeks before the Kennedy administration settled down to distribute patronage and in any event he
was ambivalent about leaving his hometown. All of his aldermen
joined him on the ticket with the exception of Jack White, whom
Telles considered politically expendable. He replaced him with
Corporation Court Judge Glenn Woodard. Although some opposition was expected, the mayor had, as the *Times* put it, "El Paso politics in the palm of his hand." Hooten even came very close to
endorsing him, noting that Telles had overcome all of his earlier
fears. "Our original apprehension that he would be dictated to by a
certain newspaper editor did not come to pass," Hooten editorialized. "We are convinced that no one has told Raymond Telles what
to do in the City Hall." The incumbent would be hard to beat for
reelection since he had made many friends and few enemies as
mayor. "We are inclined to be friendly to Mayor Telles," the *Times*
editor concluded. "We think he has done an over-all good job."[20]

Telles's future, however, was being decided less in El Paso than
in Washington. The mayor first downplayed a federal appointment and expressed irritation at the rumors surrounding his possible move to Washington. He angrily accused County Judge
Woodrow Bean of interference by sending telegrams to Washington

*Mayor Telles with Sen. Dennis Chávez of New Mexico at a
John F. Kennedy for President rally in El Paso, fall 1960.
Courtesy Raymond L. Telles*

supporting a Telles appointment. "I would appreciate it if Judge
Bean would stop interfering in my personal affairs and personal
business," Telles told a reporter. "I have not asked anyone for an
appointment." Smelling politics, he and his advisors saw in the
county judge's actions an effort to "kick Telles upstairs" and
remove him from El Paso politics or at least generate increased
opposition in the city election by candidates hoping Telles would
not run. Bean denied this and replied that the mayor had personally asked him to intervene with Sen. Ralph Yarborough of Texas
about a possible appointment in the Kennedy administration. An

angry Richard Telles even confronted Bean in a Juárez bar and after exchanging heated words, chased the judge out of the bar.[21]

Still, rumors of an impending appointment in the Kennedy administration continued to circulate. Sarah McClendon, the veteran *Times* correspondent in Washington, reported that Telles was being seriously considered as ambassador to Costa Rica.[22] In fact, that rumor was true. One day a couple of months after Kennedy had assumed office, Telles received a phone call from Kenneth O'Donnell, the president's right-hand man.

"Ray, the president is considering appointing you as ambassador to Costa Rica," O'Donnell informed Telles.

"I'm sorry Kenny," Telles responded, "but I won't even consider it."

"Why?" O'Donnell inquired.

"Many reasons," Telles explained, "but mainly because I'm still in my second term as mayor and I've already announced for a third term. I just don't want to walk away from this. I also have some special projects I want to continue."

O'Donnell seemed to accept this explanation, but a few days later Telles received another call. This time it was Vice Pres. Lyndon Johnson. Telles had known LBJ since the 1948 senatorial election when Johnson had narrowly won his first term as U.S. senator from Texas and had campaigned actively among Mexican Americans.

"Ray," LBJ said in his strong Texan accent, heavily peppered with profanities, "what in the hell is the matter with you? What do you mean turning down the president?"

Taken aback, Telles defensively retorted: "I didn't turn down anyone. This is my problem," and he proceeded to explain to the vice president what he had previously told O'Donnell.

"Well, the president wants to talk to you," Johnson concluded the conversation. "He wants you to come to Washington."

Telles agreed, especially since he had some city business to take care of in the nation's capital. However, he had no intention of going to the White House and hoped that the whole matter would just go away. But after Telles had been in Washington a few days,

Going-away festivities for Telles in south El Paso on his appointment as ambassador to Costa Rica, 24 March 1961.
Courtesy Raymond L. Telles

LBJ personally showed up at his hotel and in no uncertain terms told him: "You're going to the White House."

There Telles met with the president, Vice President Johnson, and Sen. Dennis Chávez whom Telles had known for several years and highly respected.

"I want to appoint you as ambassador to Costa Rica," President Kennedy told Telles, "but I understand that you turned down my offer."

"Mr. President," Telles courteously responded, "I didn't exactly turn it down. I just never accepted it."

Telles informed the president that he did not want to resign as mayor of El Paso. He explained that he faced no opposition in the forthcoming election and "this is the best way to run."

"Well, I agree with you," the president said.

Senator Chávez then interjected, "Raymond, don't be a fool. I've been to Costa Rica several times. It's beautiful and the people are great. You'll love it!"

"I know all that," Telles told him, "but I still have a responsibility to El Paso."

President Kennedy then said something that Telles never forgot. He told him: "You know Raymond, you're being very selfish."

This stunned Telles who responded, "Mr. President, why am I being selfish?"

"Don't you realize that you'll be the first Mexican American appointed as an ambassador? If you do a good job, you're going to open the doors for other Spanish-speaking candidates."

After some additional arm-twisting, Telles, beginning to succumb, said, "Mr. President, even if I accepted your offer, I still have certain problems I have to resolve."

"What are they?" the president wanted to know.

"I'm on my second term," Telles explained, "and I'm not going to resign. Second of all, being an ambassador takes money and I would need to have assurances that the State Department would provide sufficient funds for me to do a good job."

According to Telles, there were a few other issues, but these two were the most important to him.

President Kennedy heard him out and then concluded the meeting by saying that he would look into the issues and would get back to him.

An exhausted and bewildered Telles left the Oval Office, only to find LBJ right on his tracks. He stopped Telles and angrily almost shouted at him, "Ray, what the hell is the matter with you? Putting conditions on the president? You must be out of your mind!"

"Mr. Vice President," Telles replied, "I'm not putting on conditions. I'm just telling the president what my problems are."

"Well, you shouldn't have done that," LBJ shot back. "You don't put conditions on the president."

"Well, I'm sorry if I did that."

Telles returned to El Paso and a few days later received another phone call from O'Donnell. He secretly hoped that O'Donnell would inform him that the president could not meet all of his conditions. Instead, Telles was surprised when he was told: "The president has asked me to inform you that he has accepted all of your conditions."[23]

The news stunned Telles. He faced one of the most crucial decisions in his political career. Delfina Telles initially expressed mixed feelings about the appointment, but after some thought came to the conclusion that her husband should accept it. Telles also solicited advice from several close supporters, who in turn expressed divided opinions. Becoming ambassador would be not only a major personal triumph for him, but also a national recognition of Mexican American political contributions and capabilities. Albert Armendáriz, for example, counseled him to take the ambassadorship. "It was a natural. . . . He was entirely capable and he would do us honor up there." However, if he left El Paso he would lose his local political base and possibly jeopardize the political gains Mexican Americans had made as a result of his tenure as mayor. Indeed, a significant number of Mexican American supporters did not want Telles to leave. "Lelo" Jacques recalls organizing a meeting of between twenty and thirty people, mostly Mexican Americans, who attempted to discourage Telles from taking Kennedy's offer. If the administration were proposing the Mexico City post, it might be different, Jacques told Telles, but Costa Rica was a demotion. Perhaps, the group suspected, this was simply a plot by Telles's opponents to remove him from office since they could not defeat him any other way. Jacques and the others suggested to Telles that if he stayed for one or two more terms, in the meantime the El Paso congressional district would be redrawn to eliminate the overly conservative counties east of the city. Then Telles, with his El Paso support, could run and be elected to Congress. Even Richard Telles revealed mixed emotions. "I wanted Raymond to go up," he notes, "and yet we were losing our leader."[24]

Telles carefully deliberated on all these suggestions. In the end, however, he believed that he could not turn down the president nor the opportunity to be the first ambassador of Mexican American extraction, especially after Kennedy had agreed to all of his conditions. As Richard Telles put it: "How can you say no to John Kennedy?" The politics of status had triumphed again. Most of his ethnic constituents were delighted. They again saw in Telles's success their political arrival, except this time at the national level. They were finally receiving their due recognition. "We had never in our lives," Gabriel Navarrete remembers, "[had] an ambassador of Spanish descent from here in El Paso."[25]

Telles officially notified the city council that he would not seek reelection, but would serve out his term of office. "It is not possible for me to express my full gratitude to the people of El Paso," he stated, "and words are insufficient to tell you of the love, devotion, and pride in which I hold this community of my birth, which has twice honored me by allowing me to serve as mayor." The *New York Times* informed the rest of the nation of Telles's appointment by noting that he pronounced his name "TAY-ess, Spanish fashion. His English is the twang of a West Texan; his Spanish is flawless." Echoing Kennedy's hopes that the newly announced Alliance for Progress could successfully compete against what the new president believed to be the Communist challenge in Latin America, Telles told the *New York Times* what he believed he could accomplish in Costa Rica: "We are their friends; we are all partners in the promotion of security, for the entire hemisphere. We want to help them, but as partners. After all, we need their help as much as they need ours, if we're going to be successful in preventing the spread of Communism."[26]

Most El Pasoans expressed pride at hearing of Telles's appointment, while those who wished to see him remain in office revealed disappointment. Hooten regarded Telles's nomination as a major success for El Paso. "By naming Raymond L. Telles to be the U.S. ambassador to Costa Rica," he jokingly wrote, "President Kennedy has paid long overdue honor to the Republic of El Paso, which is geographically attached to Texas, but gets along without it very well." On the other hand, one writer to the *Times* displayed mixed feelings: "I realize it is a great honor to El Paso and to Mayor Telles, a feather in his cap . . . but I think that his real worth is right here in El Paso. He is one of the few Latin Americans that has forged ahead with his own boot straps and by so doing has set an excellent example of what other Latin-Americans can do if they have the 'will' and the 'know-how.'" "Kiko" Hernández recalls a touch of bitterness concerning the news of Telles's departure. After working hard to elevate Telles to the mayorality, "I thought he let us down." A similarly dejected Jacques thought at the time: "I knew we had lost a leader in the community."[27]

Telles's appointment also produced a flurry of activity in the city election. Not only did several candidates declare for mayor and aldermen, but members of the city council began bickering over which one of them could succeed Telles as head of the People's Ticket. Ralph Seitsinger, mayor protem during Telles's two terms, announced his willingness to be that leader, but encountered opposition from Bender and Craigo. Judge Woodard, originally selected by Telles to replace Jack White on the ticket, stated that he now wanted to run for mayor and proposed a ticket including Bender and Craigo. Hooten at the *Times* ascribed this confusion to Telles's departure: "It was a pity to see his City Council sort of disintegrate, but that often happens when a strong man steps down or leaves a post of high authority." Hoping to prevent total disintegration and to assemble a ticket that would carry on his policies, Telles personally intervened and mediated the rivalry. He endorsed Seitsinger, causing Woodard to drop out of the race and convinced Bender and Craigo to join Seitsinger in a bid for a third term. They added attorney and LULAC leader Albert Armendáriz and businessman Ray Watt to the ticket. In all, seven candidates for mayor vied in the election, along with four full tickets.[28]

Seitsinger and his aldermanic candidates called on voters to reaffirm their support for the People's Ticket and sought to make the election a referendum on the Telles years. The top plank in their platform read: "To continue the progressive policies of Mayor

*Pres. John F. Kennedy and Telles as newly appointed
ambassador to Costa Rica, April 1961.
Courtesy Raymond L. Telles*

Raymond Telles's administration and the principles for representing all the people in the city government." Telles did not campaign
for the Seitsinger ticket, but made known his support for it plus
provided brother Richard's political network to turn out the Mexican
American vote. Political commentators considered the top mayoral
candidates to be Seitsinger and Ernest Ponce, Mexican American
former alderman, with arch-conservative Mrs. Julia Breck, a dark
horse. The *Herald-Post* noted, however, that the Seitsinger ticket
might be hurt by the recent police examination scandal. Yet with
Richard Telles's help plus his own Lower Valley base, Seitsinger
won a plurality but not a majority with six other candidates running.
Mrs. Breck finished second and forced Seitsinger into a run-off.
Only Ted Bender of the People's Ticket won outright.[29]

In the runoff, Mrs. Breck attempted to make an issue of Richard Telles and questioned the integrity of Mexican American voters. She appealed to El Pasoans to "Break The Machine With Breck—The Only Candidate Who Can Eliminate Rubber Stamp 'Yes Man' type of City Government In El Paso." She accused the Telles administration of providing favors for only a select few and of running what she termed a "village type administration." The People's Ticket, she charged, relied on "controlled voters" rather than "qualified voters." Her hard-hitting campaign proved effective in Anglo precincts, but at the same time stimulated voter turnout in the southern ones and in the Lower Valley, which voted heavily for Seitsinger. With 52.3 percent of the vote, Seitsinger won but failed to carry his entire ticket. Both Craigo and Armendáriz lost close races. While voters in the northern Anglo precincts did not necessarily accept the election as a referendum on Raymond Telles, Mexican American voters did. Those in south and southeast El Paso and Ysleta—Telles's strongholds—gave Seitsinger 4,843 votes (87 percent of the vote) to Mrs. Breck's 735. Without Telles's endorsement and Richard's aid, Seitsinger would not have won.[30]

Pleased with Seitsinger's victory, Mayor Telles prepared to depart El Paso. Before he did, his constituents showered him with affection and gifts. It was a particularly poignant time for Mexican Americans. They had struggled for years against second-class citizenship and, by electing Telles, believed they had finally been accepted as full-fledged Americans. Telles was their proof. He was their status symbol. His elevation to ambassador lifted their ethnic political recognition from the local to the national level. Still, Mexican Americans could not help but feel a sense of loss. They might recapture the mayor's office again, but there could never be another Raymond Telles—the perfect candidate in their eyes. Saddened but proud, they honored him by staging a parade through south El Paso. From San José Hall several thousand Mexican Americans, led by the Bowie High School band, escorted the mayor to a large rally at Armijo Park. On the way, they stopped at 918 South St. Vrain, where he had been born. Here, the Rev. José López blessed the house and presented Telles a special papal blessing from Pope John XXIII. "I thank God for His goodness in enabling me to serve my people," Telles emotionally responded to his supporters. "I am thankful for the people being so good to me and my family."[31]

A series of receptions and parties followed during the next few days. "When he departs," his longtime political ally, Ed Pooley, wrote, "he will be accompanied by his hometown's best wishes for a happy, successful life as a diplomat." Always the battler, Pooley could not resist using Telles's departure as a reason to favor widespread Spanish-language instruction in the city schools. The editor stressed that among the new ambassador's assets was his ability to speak Spanish well. "Not every youngster who learns Spanish is going to be an ambassador, like Mayor Telles," Pooley concluded. "But equipped with the language, thousands of young El Pasoans can acquire greater knowledge and understanding of Latin America."[32]

In his last official act as mayor, Telles swore in Seitsinger and the aldermen. "Although you are physically leaving El Paso today," Ken Flynn, speaking for city hall reporters, emphasized, "I don't think you will ever leave the hearts of your fellow El Pasoans whom you have served so well." One day later in Washington, Telles formally became ambassador to Costa Rica. "I am extremely gratefully to President Kennedy," he commented at the State Department. "I certainly hope I will be a credit to the administration. I am very proud to be a part of the Kennedy administration and a member of the Kennedy team." With his wife, Delfina, and his two young daughters, Cynthia and Patricia, Raymond Telles entered the New Frontier. "I felt that I was in a position to help my people," he recalls of his new adventure in public service,

> that I really had the opportunity being the first Mexican American to be named. I felt that just like I had done as county clerk that I would open the possibilities as mayor and now here I was an ambassador opening up the way for other people to be appointed. And I'm not saying that I was totally responsible, but I think it helped and, as a consequence, after that we had several.[33]

CHAPTER SIX

Mr. Ambassador

Although it was rumored from time to time that he would next be named ambassador to Mexico, Raymond Telles served in Costa Rica for six years (1961–1967). This was an unusually long tenure for an ambassador in any one country. It reflected, however, his effectiveness there. Despite strong anti-American sentiment in Central America, Telles became a highly popular figure in Costa Rica and a close personal friend of that country's leading political figures. In his new job, he was greatly aided by his wife, Delfina, who played an active charitable and social role as the ambassador's wife. Moreover, their two daughters, rather than attending the more exclusive, English-language American school in the capital city of San José, instead went to Spanish-speaking Costa Rican schools.

Without question the most memorable moment in this period was President Kennedy's visit to Costa Rica in March of 1963, just a few months before his assassination. He had earlier visited Mexico and some of the South American countries to promote his Latin American policy, the Alliance for Progress, as well as his containment policy toward revolutionary Cuba; however, he had

Ambassador Telles and family at official residence
in San José, Costa Rica, circa early 1960s.
Courtesy El Paso Times

not visited Central America. Telles believed that it was important for the president to do so and encouraged such a visit. Kennedy agreed and it was arranged for him to meet with all of the heads of state of the Central American countries in San José.

The president stayed with Telles and his family in the ambassador's residence. To accommodate Kennedy's chronic back problem, local craftsmen were engaged to build both a special bed and chair for him. Although specific meetings with the Central American leaders had been prearranged, no other itinerary had been organized. For his part, Telles believed that the president should visit the national university in San José and address the students who represented the leaders of the future. Kennedy and his advisors demurred, fearing Communist-inspired protests.

President Kennedy on a visit to Costa Rica
with Telles family, March 1963.
Courtesy Raymond L. Telles

"No, I can't do that," the president told Telles. "The State Department says no. My security people say no. My advisors say no. Everyone is saying no, except you."

Telles attempted to assure Kennedy that he knew the university well and had himself often met with students there. He did not believe that any problems would arise. Kennedy remained skeptical but finally agreed to do so.

"Well, Ray, I'm going, but remember you're the guy who's pushing me into this."

"O.K., Mr. President," Telles responded, suddenly realizing that the weight of responsibility for this visit rested on his shoulders.

Kennedy and his aides, accompanied by Telles, flew by helicopter onto the university grounds where they transferred into an awaiting car that would drive them to where Kennedy would speak. They were greeted by thousands of students who wanted to see and to touch the young American president. "If they really wanted to kill the president, they could have done it there," Telles notes. "And the president didn't help any. He got out of the car and walked into the crowd."

Kennedy's visit and the speech in which he, among other things, conceded that the United States had not always applied its democratic principles to Latin America, proved to be a great success. While some red flags were raised by radical students, they were quickly torn down by others. On returning to the embassy on the helicopter, a pleased Kennedy turned to Telles.

"It's a damn good thing everything went well down there."

"Mr. President, don't you think I know it," his relieved host replied.

Besides the appearance at the university, Telles also wanted Kennedy to pay a visit to the national cathedral in San José. He told the president that the archbishop had specifically invited him. But Kennedy again at first objected.

"No, you already dragged me to the university. You should be satisfied."

"But Mr. President," Telles persisted. "There are three things that are important here. First of all, the archbishop of Costa Rica is a very important person. Second of all, when you visited Mexico, you went to the cathedral there."

"So what?" Kennedy stated.

"Well, that's something you should think about."

Telles, however, had one more angle to work. He reminded Kennedy that 19 March was the feast of San José and that his father's Catholic feast day was that of St. Joseph or San José. This seemed to impress Kennedy and he finally agreed to go to the cathedral. On the day of his visit, thousands of Costa Ricans showed up and were visibly moved when the American Catholic president knelt to pray.

Telles, at the encouragement of his wife, was further successful in getting Kennedy to spend some time at a local children's hospital.

The president had no objections. Visibly affected by the children and the hospital's need for new equipment, Kennedy personally wrote out a check for $125,000.

At the San José meeting of Central American leaders, Telles also recalls an informal conversation at a reception when Anastacio Somoza, the right-wing dictator of Nicaragua, in a somewhat lighthearted yet serious vein asked President Kennedy to do him the favor of appointing Telles as ambassador to Nicaragua. Kennedy was noncommittal, but after Somoza left, Telles turned to him and said: "Mr. President, I want you to do *me* a favor. Please don't ever send me to Nicaragua." The president laughed in agreement and instead informed Telles that he was considering appointing him ambassador to Mexico.

Telles's relationship with Kennedy, although short-lived due to the president's assassination, was a strong one. Whenever Kennedy toured the Southwest, he would recall Telles to the United States. During the delicate negotiations concerning the Chamizal Treaty that would return a portion of disputed land in El Paso to Mexico, Kennedy called on Telles to work out some of the details affecting the residents who would have to be relocated.

On a trip to California with Telles aboard the presidential plane, the president told him that a problem had arisen because some of the people—all Mexican Americans—whose property would be affected by the Chamizal Treaty had raised objections to the transfer.

"You being from El Paso," the president told him, "I thought you might know what the problem is all about."

Telles did not know but suggested that Air Force One stop in El Paso and that he would check into the problem and then report back to the president. Kennedy agreed and Telles visited with the Chamizal residents, who informed him, while they had no objections to the transfer of the property, the federal government was offering them market value which was lower than the replacement value they desired. Telles agreed with them and reported this back to Kennedy. On learning about the residents' concerns, the president responded: "Is that the problem?" He instructed his aides to see to it that the people affected be given replacement value. Kennedy never lived to see the Chamizal Treaty completed, but Telles returned to El Paso for the final signing ceremony 28 October 1967 by Pres. Lyndon Johnson and Pres. Gustavo Díaz Ordaz of Mexico.

Telles recalls that the death of President Kennedy was one of the saddest and most emotional events of his life. He had in fact been invited to join the president in Texas, including the tragic visit to Dallas. However, the ambassador was locked up in particular negotiations with the Costa Rican government and felt that he could not leave this business. Kennedy agreed. The date 22 November 1963 is forever etched in Telles's memory:

> I will never forget that Friday. I had left my office around noon to return to the ambassador's residence for lunch. When I arrived, I was told that a very important telephone call from the White House was waiting for me at the office. I immediately returned. The call was to advise me that the president had been shot in Dallas. I was also asked to inform the president of Costa Rica and that they would call me in a couple of hours to let me know the president's condition. Approximately two hours later, I received the second call informing me that President Kennedy had died. It would be very difficult to explain and describe the terrible feeling that traveled through my entire body. I had a difficult time believing what I had been told. I asked the White House if someone was kidding or playing a joke. I was assured that unfortunately those were the true facts. When the news was made public in Costa Rica, the people were out in the streets openly and loudly crying. They loved President Kennedy. You would have thought that he had been their president. It was rather strange that on that same Friday, I received a letter from the president telling me that he was sorry that I could not be with him in Texas, but that he agreed that it was best for me to continue my work in Costa Rica. President Kennedy also said in his letter that he wanted to talk to me the next time I was in Washington. What he wanted to talk to me about, I will never know.

Ambassador Telles with people of Costa Rica, circa early 1960s.
Courtesy El Paso Times

After President Kennedy's assassination, Telles, as was customary for all political appointees, offered to resign his post to allow the new president to make his own appointments. Johnson, however, refused the resignation and kept him on as his ambassador to Costa Rica. While Telles was willing to continue serving in the small Central American country, he also hoped that he might be appointed ambassador to Mexico someday, as Kennedy had hinted to him. Instead, Johnson later offered him the opportunity to become the U.S. representative to a newly formed U.S.-Mexico Border Commission to examine joint border problems, retaining his rank as ambassador.

Telles was flattered at this offer but still hoped for the post in Mexico. At a meeting in Washington with LBJ to discuss the new appointment, he could not help but bring up the issue of the ambassadorship to Mexico. He asked Johnson if he knew of Kennedy's intention of sending him there. The president in a stern fashion responded, "Oh, yes, I knew that. But don't you understand that there's a new president now, a new administration and that I have other commitments?"

Telles understood what Johnson meant and did not pursue the matter. Instead, he agreed to head the U.S.-Mexico Border Commission. Headquartered in Washington, he occupied that post from 1967 to 1969 when Pres. Richard Nixon dismissed him.[1]

Although Telles had been away for several years, El Pasoans still remembered him with fondness. Occasionally stories circulated that he would return and run for Congress. During his years in Costa Rica, he had lost contact with local politics, but still yearned to once again serve his community. Finally, in 1969 he believed the time had come to permanently return to El Paso and electoral politics. He hoped to reignite the "Telles magic" and announced that he would challenge the three-term Democratic representative from the Sixteenth Congressional District, Richard White.[2]

His decision to run for office again was based on three conditions that he believed were strikingly similar to those when he had run for mayor in 1957. First, he believed, as he had nine years earlier, that he could do the job. After years of federal service, he possessed contacts in Washington that would allow him to serve El Paso better than White. "I was well established in Washington," he recalls thinking. "I knew a good number of the members of Congress . . . and I felt I could continue my service to my community and certainly to the country in that position." Second, as in 1957, he considered his opponent vulnerable. White had been elected three times, but Telles believed the congressman had not proven to be a real "Great Society" Democrat and had been lax in protecting El Paso's interests. The people would welcome a change. Finally, with brother Richard's encouragement, he banked on the Mexican American vote that had elected him to office as mayor. The old coalition could be revived.[3]

Ambassador Telles with Pres. Adolfo López Mateos of Mexico
and Pres. Lyndon B. Johnson at the initial signing of the
Chamizal Treaty, El Paso–Juárez, 25 September 1964.
Mrs. Lyndon (Lady Bird) Johnson is on the left in the rear.
Courtesy Raymond L. Telles

Unfortunately for Telles, 1970 was not 1957. Few disputed his credentials to be an excellent congressman, but he faced a formidable opponent. Telles attempted to undercut White's support by leveling various charges against him. He called attention, for example, to White's failure to endorse several Great Society welfare issues. These included voting against urban renewal and the Model Cities appropriation, the 1966 Civil Rights Act, open housing, and antipoverty funds. Telles noted that if elected he would not only support these issues, but do more than White on inflation, health care, social security, education, and a host of other social measures. Moreover, he charged that White had also proved to be an ineffective representative. Telles specifically accused White of not being influential enough to prevent cutbacks in El Paso military installations. The congressman had been away on a trip to the South Pacific while Congress debated installing a new missile system in the El Paso area. The city failed to obtain the agency and Telles blamed White. He likewise attributed to White's ineptness the closing in 1965 of Biggs Air Force Base and El Paso's inability to acquire a defense language school. "Is this the record of a man who really knows his way around Washington?" Telles asked. "I say it is a combination of lack of good judgment, a lack of influence in the right quarters, poor strategy, poor timing, the story of too little and too late."[4]

Telles further charged White with unethical practices such as using taxpayers' money to mail out campaign literature and employing too many part-time employees on his congressional payroll. In general, Telles concluded, White lacked leadership qualities. The former mayor contrasted himself with White by citing his long history of public service and insisting that he would exert leadership in Washington. El Pasoans would be electing both a representative and a statesman. "Elect Raymond Telles to Congress," his political ad read. "Aggressive Statesmanship For A Decade of Progress."[5]

Despite his opponent's aggressive style—unusual for his gentlemanly demeanor—the incumbent astutely counterattacked and neutralized Telles's charges. White had not supported all Great Society programs, but he had endorsed enough to benefit from the reform aura of LBJ's administration. This proved to be especially important as White courted Mexican Americans concerned about issues such as housing, food stamps, and job training. In addition, White had impressed constituents by being able to acquire funding for particular El Paso projects including the Chamizal Memorial Highway and the Chamizal Memorial Park. He admitted that military cuts had affected the city but boasted of acquiring $17.5 million for construction of the new William Beaumont Army Hospital and the Vietnamese Language School at Biggs Air Force Base. White especially reminded voters of his position on the House

Armed Services Committee, so essential for the community's reliance on military spending. The congressman disputed Telles's charge of laxity and absenteeism by obtaining from Rep. Mendel Rivers, chairman of the House Armed Services Committee, a statement attesting to White's services to the committee. He denied unethical practices in his Washington office and, instead, portrayed Telles as having limited status there. "Mr. Telles says he has influence in Washington," White stressed. "I must question this influence he might have in an administration which has already relieved him of his position on the Commission on Development and Friendship [Border Commission] and replaced him with a man from San Antonio." Telles might have had key contacts in the past, White conceded, but his sponsors in Washington were now gone. "His entire advertising campaign is built around pictures of him and Pres. John F. Kennedy and Pres. Lyndon Johnson. . . . However, the plain facts are that neither President Kennedy nor President Johnson are in Washington any longer."[6]

Unable to develop effective issues against White, Telles hoped to revitalize his past political influence and the friendships he had developed while mayor. Yet, influential Anglos who had supported him after his election in 1957 saw no necessity to do so now with White in Washington. Although some Mexican American leaders such as Alfredo Montoya of the Steelworkers' Union and city alderman Sal Berroteran supported Telles, he discovered that time had also eroded his Mexican American base. Many still rallied to the Telles banner but not with the same enthusiasm and energy exerted in the past. His peers had grown older with him and had benefited to an extent from the political breakthroughs of his administration. No other Mexican American had been elected as mayor since Telles's departure, but several won posts as city councilmen, county commissioners, including Richard Telles, and state representatives. In addition, many more now served in fairly influential city and county administrative positions. In all, Mexican Americans were not as "hungry" for political representation as they had been in 1957 nor did they feel themselves as much outsiders to the political process. "The fire was out," recalls "Kiko" Hernández.[7]

Opening of Telles for Congress headquarters,
with Gilbert Roland, El Paso, March 1970.
Courtesy Raymond L. Telles

Many believed that Mexican Americans had achieved political status—they could no longer be denied representation in El Paso—and now had to turn to obtaining economic parity with Anglos. Some, while emotionally attached to Telles, simply believed he had no chance of defeating White. Gabriel Navarrete remembers telling both Raymond and Richard that many voters no longer knew who Raymond Telles was. A few others still harbored resentments about his departure in 1961. Hernández said, "I was still hurt." The lack of enthusiasm among his old *compañeros* hurt Telles both organizationally and financially. He recalls acquiring promises of campaign contributions, but being unable to collect. "Well, yes, I promised you $1,000," someone would tell him, "but business is not so good, things are looking pretty bad." Consequently, he ran an underfinanced campaign that limited his exposure, especially on television.[8]

Telles could not even rely on the *Herald-Post*. Pooley had died and the newspaper had become more conservative. Both daily newspapers endorsed White. "With all due respect to Mr. Telles," Robert E. Lee, the new editor of the *Herald-Post*, wrote:

> we feel that Congressman White deserves to be re-elected to office and we strongly support his candidacy. We see no reason to depose a good and effective man simply to install, in his place, another man who may also be good and effective. There is nothing to gain and much to lose, particularly when the matter of congressional seniority is considered.[9]

Unable to generate enthusiastic support from his former supporters, Telles failed even more among the younger generation—the Chicanos. Children or teenagers when Telles served as mayor, Chicanos only vaguely remembered him. Instead, they saw Telles as an outsider who, along with others of his generation, seemed out of step with their own more militant demands for political and cultural self-determination—"Chicano Power." Age and politics separated Telles from the activists. "People tend to forget, you know," Telles remembers of his unsuccessful encounters with Chicano youth:

> But more than that the young people that were, let's say, anywhere from ten to fifteen years old when I was mayor. Now, after ten years they were grown up men, but they really didn't know who Telles was. . . . No, you asked their parents and sure they knew me and they were all for me and they were willing to vote for me and all that. But these young people who didn't know me, I had quite a bit of a problem with them 'cause I would meet them and I would say, here's what I did when I was mayor and the reaction was, "Well, what have you done for us today, what have you done for us lately?"[10]

Richard White further eroded Telles's support base with his ability to acquire Mexican American endorsements. He accomplished this not only by voting for particular welfare measures, but by assiduously maintaining contact with Mexican American voters. The incumbent reminded them that he had sponsored the proclamation of National LULAC Week, had endorsed the establishment of the Cabinet Committee on Opportunities for Spanish-speaking People, and had provided Mexican American representation on the Equal Employment Opportunity Commission. He also astutely appointed Mrs. Félix Hinojosa as his co-campaign manager. "I have known Congressman White since before he was elected to Congress," she stated, "and I personally believe that he has represented and served the people of his district well—rich, poor, black, white, and Mexican American, all alike." In a significant blow to the Telles campaign, the local Mexican American Political Association (MAPA) endorsed White. Never one for publicly exploiting his ethnic background, Telles even faced unfair criticism for dividing Mexican Americans. "Over and over Mr. Telles says that if he is elected he will help the Mexican American people," Mrs. Luis Pérez wrote to the *Herald-Post*. "Congressman Richard C. White represents all the people of the 16th District, not just certain groups. Mr. Telles is dividing his own people—the Mexican American people."[11]

Lacking organization and money, Telles could draw on only brother Richard's political talents. However, while Richard could still deliver the hard-core Mexican American south side, he could not provide the spontaneity that had sparked the 1957 campaign and led to victory. Not even the appearance of movie star and former El Pasoan Gilbert Roland on his behalf could stir much enthusiasm. Helping to open Telles's campaign headquarters, Roland endorsed the candidate and proclaimed him "capable of doing the job in Washington." Richard Telles admits that as much as he wanted his brother to win, his political instincts told him that Raymond stood no chance against White. Yet he believed that Raymond could still benefit by using the campaign to keep his name in the news and hopefully regain a position in the federal government. To compound the problem, Mexican Americans were dispersed now throughout the city and many had become more occupationally mobile and secure. Hence, they were harder to organize politically, not susceptible to Richard's influence, and less willing to vote along strict ethnic lines. "But the fact that you are Mexican does not necessarily get you elected by the people of Mexican extraction," Luciano Santoscoy explained the voting patterns of 1970. Mexican Americans still supported candidates of their own, but less for status and more for what these politicians could deliver in return. Many were not sure that Telles could help them and believed White had already proven himself. Consequently, Telles could only fall back on the memory of his 1957 victory and his years as mayor and as ambassador. His supporters appealed to the memories of the past in calling for his election. In the end, the politics of nostalgia was not enough.[12]

Telles experienced the only electoral defeat of his career and lost almost two to one in El Paso and exactly by that spread in the rest of the congressional district. "In El Paso the biggest surprise of the day," the *Herald-Post* editorialized, "was the margin of victory by which incumbent Rep. Richard C. White won the renomination to his 16th District Congressional seat over former Mayor Raymond Telles." White carried all 12 counties in the district and totaled 40,147 votes to Telles's 20,016. In El Paso County, White surpassed Telles, 28,537 to 15,109. Telles won only 24 precincts out of 85. His support came from the old Mexican American belt of south and southeast El Paso with a smattering of Lower Valley precincts. Telles not only failed to win certain northern Mexican American precincts such as Precinct 6, the old Morehead School on Arizona and Campbell Streets, where he lost by more than 3,000 votes, but he attracted few votes from the predominantly Anglo precincts. He took his loss in stride, having sensed defeat before the election. "I could understand why it happened and I think that was the reason why I wasn't too bitter or disappointed."[13]

Telles left El Paso soon after the election and returned to Washington where President Nixon appointed him as a Democrat to the bipartisan Equal Employment Opportunity Commission. He served there five years until 1976. Telles desired involvement in inter-American affairs once more and after one year as a private consultant, accepted a position under the new Carter administration as head of the Inter-American Development Bank in El Salvador. In that civil-war-torn country, Telles experienced some difficult and potential life-threatening situations. On one occasion his official car was stopped by guerrilla troops who assaulted Telles's driver and firebombed the vehicle. Fortunately, the ambassador was not in the car. Twice Telles, while visiting development programs in the countryside, found himself surrounded by rebels armed with guns and machetes. They accused him of being a spy. Again luck was on Telles's side as he escaped unharmed after reminding his accusers that he was supporting programs that "helped your people."[14]

Following Pres. Jimmy Carter's defeat by Ronald Reagan in 1980, Telles felt that he now had few friends in Washington. He longed to return to El Paso. Consequently, in April of 1982, he accepted the position of senior vice president of the International Division of First Financial Enterprises, an El Paso-based firm. The former mayor's specific appointment concerned the banking operations of First Financial. Raymond Telles had come home to stay. "I felt that we had been away 21 years," he observed. "My family was here. Delfina's family was here. I felt the need to return. I just wanted to come back home."[15]

In private business for the first time in his career, he enjoyed significant economic success. "In naming Raymond Telles to direct the expansion of our financial services beyond international boundaries," Maury Page Kemp, the chairman of the board and founder of First Financial, announced, "we share the confidence in his abilities demonstrated by the six U.S. presidents whom he has served."[16]

According to Telles, Kemp had been a longtime friend and supporter. In addition to the bank, Kemp also owned and operated three insurance companies. Telles's appointment and responsibility, however, was only with the bank.[17]

Yet despite his new business career, upon returning to El Paso he still encountered rumors that he would resume his political career by running for mayor again. Indeed, some voices in the community, especially many Mexican Americans who recalled or knew of his earlier political successes, called on the former mayor to throw his hat in the ring for city office during the 1980s. Although by that decade, Mexican Americans represented about 70 percent of the city's population of almost half a million and now constituted majorities in both the city council and the county government, they still faced difficulties in electing a mayor from their ranks. Since Telles's departure in 1961, only one other Mexican American, Ray Salazar, had held that office. Salazar served from 1977 to 1979, but was defeated in his reelection effort. Despite these setbacks, at least Mexican Americans in El Paso could claim to have elected one of their own as mayor of a large southwestern city well before others. Being proud of this distinction, they and other El Pasoans were particularly irked when the national media touted the election of Henry Cisneros as mayor of San Antonio in 1981 as representing the first successful election of a Mexican American to lead a major southwestern urban community. El Pasoans were not impressed; they had done it in 1957 and under more difficult circumstances than those which faced Cisneros. Moreover, El Pasoans were disturbed by the notion that the national media did not consider El Paso to be a major southwestern city.[18]

Hence, if there was still a political hunger among Mexican Americans in El Paso, it was to recapture the mayoral slot. Difficulties for Mexican American interests in accomplishing this consisted of divisions and rivalries among political leaders, the lack of an effective and well-organized voting bloc due to their further fragmentation throughout the city and the increase of political interest groups, and, finally, the lack of adequate financial resources among their candidates to run well-financed campaigns against more economically potent Anglo candidates.

Consequently some Mexican Americans, and even some Anglo Americans, believed that Telles's return might just represent the missing link in recapturing the mayor's office. Columnist Joe Olvera writing in the *El Paso Times* called on Telles to consider running in the 1989 election. Olvera felt Telles was the only candidate who could unite what he called "a divided city." "Who else can generate respect and confidence throughout the entire city of El Paso?"

Olvera stressed. "Telles can reach people with his decency, his charisma and his dedication and commitment to making our city the best in the state and the nation."[19]

Honored and pleased that some still considered him a viable candidate, Telles, although tempted to run, declined these overtures while still holding out the possibility of a future campaign. "It's very nice to think that people would think of me as a potential candidate," Telles told a reporter as late as 1993, "but it's out of the question at this moment. I would consider it only if I thought that there's a crisis."[20]

Unfortunately for him, the crisis proved to be less in the city than in his own personal and business affairs. Indeed, since his last try for elective office in 1970, Telles had experienced his first major personal crisis. In 1976, while a member of the Equal Employment Opportunity Commission, he and his wife, Delfina, were indicted by a federal grand jury for allegedly employing an undocumented domestic from Costa Rica in their home in the Washington, D.C., area and for paying her wages lower than the minimum stipulated by the Department of Labor for live-in domestics. According to both Raymond and Delfina Telles, the charges were false and misleading. Mrs. Telles had been asked by a friend in Costa Rica to host a young woman in their Maryland home who wanted to come to the United States to learn English. Mrs. Telles agreed and she arranged for the woman to enter the country with a student visa. After a few months, this arrangement proved untenable because, according to Telles, the woman would not abide by certain house rules set down by the Telleses. Apparently believing that her hosts were going to send her back to Costa Rica, in retaliation she complained to immigration officials that she had been exploited as a domestic servant. After investigations by both the Immigration and Naturalization Service (INS) and the FBI, the U.S. Attorney's Office in Washington concluded that the Telleses were innocent of the charges of harboring and exploiting an undocumented domestic. In a 7 April 1976 letter Brian W. Shaughnessy, an assistant U.S. attorney, wrote to Telles:

The information gathered by the Federal Bureau of Investigation and applicable law have been thoroughly reviewed. From that review we have concluded that further action on this matter by the United States Attorney's Office is not warranted.[21]

Unfortunately for the Telleses, the issue was not laid to rest. It became embroiled, he says, in the presidential campaign politics of 1976. After agreeing to serve as chair of the Hispanic-outreach efforts of the Democratic party, he was informed by the INS that it had resumed its investigation of the case of the Costa Rican woman. This was done in spite of the earlier decision by the U.S. Attorney's Office to drop the case. Telles believes that the INS was acting at the behest of Republican party officials who wished to disrupt the efforts of the Democratic party, through Telles's leadership, to gain Hispanic voters. Not able to get indictments against the Telleses either in Washington or in Maryland, where U.S. attorneys concluded no evidence existed for any charges, the INS finally succeeded in getting a federal grand jury in Virginia to indict the couple.

While confident that the evidence would once again confirm their innocence, Telles came under extreme pressures by the INS and the U.S. Attorney's Office in Virginia. As a result, he resigned from his Democratic party appointment in the 1976 campaign. Despite Mrs. Telles's failing health at the time, prosecutors threatened to call her as a witness against the ambassador and to proceed on a separate trial for her. Wishing to avoid further anguish for his wife, Telles finally agreed to a suggestion by the INS that he accept a plea bargain that involved charges being dropped against his wife in exchange for his admission of guilt to lesser misdemeanor charges and the paying of a fine. To stop the harassment of his family, Telles accepted this arrangement.[22]

Although this was a temporary embarrassment for the former El Paso mayor and ambassador, he did not suffer long-range consequences. In fact, in El Paso where the employment of undocumented domestics was a historic practice, most residents discounted the importance of the charges. Some even organized a "Raymond Telles Legal Defense Fund" to raise money for him.[23]

The undocumented domestic case, however, paled by comparison with a much more troubling crisis for Telles which broke in the late 1980s. Beginning with lawsuits in 1989 and culminating in indictments against key figures within Kemp's insurance companies, charges were publicly brought forth alleging that these firms had swindled millions of dollars, especially from investors in Mexico. These investors from Juárez and Chihuahua alleged that they had placed their money with Kemp's insurance companies largely because of their contacts with Telles and their trust in him. Hurt by the peso devaluation that rocked the Mexican economy in the early 1980s, wealthy Mexicans were seeking to send their fortunes out of the country. What these investors did not understand, however, was that Telles had nothing to do with the insurance companies. His job was to attract Mexicans to invest in Kemp's bank, First Financial Savings and Loan Association, which had several branches in El Paso. In time some of these investors also put money into Kemp's insurance companies—First Service Life Insurance, Knickerbocker Insurance Company, and Security Southwest Life—where they could receive twice the interest rate that they could get with the bank. The confusion that unfortunately linked Telles to the eventual problems of the insurance companies was that some of his Mexican clients would inquire of him the location of the insurance companies. He would inform them that these operations were on the other side of the building but on the same floor as the bank. Because there were no Spanish-speaking financial officers in the insurance companies who could explain in Spanish the intricate details of the company's insurance policies, Telles at times interpreted for the Mexicans, most of whom he had known for years. But he insists that he never advised them about insurance policies because, among other things, he was totally unfamiliar with these operations. Moreover, he would be hurting his own work which was to get the Mexicans to deposit their money in the savings and loan association. His responsibility was with the bank and not with the insurance companies.[24]

What the Mexican investors further did not know was that their investments in Kemp's insurance companies, specifically in annuities, were not protected against losses. This lack of protection stemmed from the fact that under Texas state insurance laws, foreigners who invested in Texas licensed insurance companies were not covered for liability. What made matters worse was that First Service Life Insurance—the main source of deposits—was not even licensed in Texas to begin with, but had been licensed in the British West Indies. Hence, not only were the Mexican investors not covered with respect to losses but neither were any other investors. This was not the case, however, in Kemp's bank where Telles worked. Here depositors—both U.S. citizens and noncitizens—were insured up to $100,000 by the Federal Deposit Insurance Corporation (FDIC).[25]

When Kemp's financial empire crumbled due to bad investments in the 1980s and his insurance companies were taken over by state regulators, his investors, primarily the Mexicans, lost almost all of their savings and were not covered by any liability laws. Losses amounted to more than $30 million. Kemp's growing financial problems, including pressures on the bank, led Telles to resign from his position in 1988. That same year the bank was declared insolvent.[26]

One year later, 30 Mexican investors filed a federal lawsuit against Kemp, Telles, and other officers of the insurance companies. They claimed that they had never been told by Telles that their investments were risky because they were not covered for losses and that First Service Life was not even properly licensed in Texas. Instead, the Mexicans alleged Telles had assured them that they were protected by law and by Kemp's own financial resources. Although the Mexicans confused the former mayor's relationship with the insurance companies, the fact was that Telles was not an officer of those operations. An examination of the governing structure of the insurance companies nowhere reveals his name. By contrast, he was prominently listed as a senior vice president of Kemp's bank. Telles believes that many of these Mexican investors were further confused about his role and position due to efforts by certain elements of the El Paso press to implicate him in the developing scandal by suggesting to these investors that the source of their problems lay with Telles.[27]

For his part, Telles denied any knowledge of the unlicensed nature of the insurance companies or that Mexican investors were not protected. "I had no reason to know," he points out. Although the Mexicans claimed, as would later indictments against Telles, that he had unlawfully operated as an insurance agent and he was not licensed as an agent, he denied ever functioning in that role or working for the insurance companies. Telles countered that his main responsibility as an officer of Kemp's bank was to inform prospective investors about the bank, First Financial Savings and Loan, but that he had nothing to do with the insurance companies. "Naturally, they are looking for somebody to blame, and I can understand that," Telles told a reporter. "I don't blame them, I'd be frustrated, too. But as far as my role in this thing, we served in the international department of a bank. We served only as an information center, and these people came to me because they knew me."[28]

Telles's lack of connection with the insurance companies was corroborated by Kemp himself who in a press release in 1988 wrote: "The allegations against Raymond Telles are particularly distressing to me. I believe he is a man of impeccable integrity who would not knowingly mislead or misrepresent the facts to anyone. I have great respect for him. His whole life has been spent in service to others and he has been a tremendous asset to the community and our nation. To my knowledge he has never received any compensation or benefits of any kind from the insurance companies. He has never been an officer, director, employee, or paid agent of any of the insurance companies."[29]

Although nothing eventually came of the lawsuits, one year later Kemp and Telles were indicted by an El Paso County grand jury on charges of violating Texas state securities laws. The indictments followed an investigation into Kemp's insurance companies by the State Securities Board. Telles had been requested to appear before the grand jury, but on the advice of his attorney had chosen not to do so on the argument that this might be used further by the district attorney to build a case against him. Instead, he chose to assert his Fifth Amendment rights against self-incrimination. He believes that in retrospect this was bad advice on the part of his attorney and that had he testified and proven that he had no connections with the insurance companies, he would not have been indicted. He further believes that the indictment was politically motivated to enhance the career of District Attorney Steve Simmons who was running for reelection and who, according to Telles, believed that prosecuting both Kemp and Telles would aid his campaign. Simmons miscalculated, Telles notes, and lost the election.[30]

To further complicate matters, in 1991 a state grand jury issued conspiracy indictments against Kemp and several other prominent El Paso businessmen, lawyers, and even other corporations, such as the El Paso Electric Company, who had been associated with Kemp's investments and who, unlike the Mexican investors, benefited from the investments by others in the unlicensed insurance firm. Telles, himself, was not indicted, but was subpoenaed one year later to testify at the trial proceedings held in Midland, Texas.[31]

At Midland, Telles under oath explained to the state prosecutors that he had no connection with Kemp's insurance companies, that he was totally unfamiliar with the licensing conditions of those companies, and that he had never served as an agent for those companies with the Mexican investors. When it became apparent at the Midland proceedings that Telles, despite the accusations of some of the investors and allegations in the press, had nothing to do with the insurance scandal, the district attorney in El Paso dropped the indictment against him. He concluded that Telles was innocent of any charges connected with the insurance companies. In a letter written to Telles's attorney two years later, Charles E. McDonald, one of the special prosecutors in the indictment , wrote:

> Before dismissing the charges against Mr. Telles, I questioned him at length regarding his involvement in the sale of annuities by First Financial to Mexican Nationals. Based on my interview

with Mr. Telles, I concluded that no probable cause existed and strongly recommended to Mr. [Andrew] Thomas [assistant district attorney] that the State dismiss Mr. Telles. After reviewing my notes with Mr. Thomas, he agreed with my conclusion that no probable cause existed and agreed to dismiss the charges.[32]

Following his testimony, Telles told reporters that his defense had cost him more than $100,000 and had wiped out his life's savings. Still, the former mayor expressed relief that this crisis now appeared to be over even if it had taken a considerable toll on him and his family.

"I feel terrible," he noted. "I think my reputation and my character were damaged. While I know that people who were my friends and people who knew me didn't believe it, I am not sure about others.

"It's been quite an ordeal. It hasn't been easy because people go by and they know you and they look at you, and you are practically reading their minds: 'Oh, oh, there goes Telles, who's been indicted.'

"I figure it's one of those adversities that happens to everyone in life. Certainly, I'm not happy about that. But I'm not embittered. My belief in the good Lord, who has been present all the time I have been going through this, has helped me maintain composure."[33]

Looking back on this unfortunate incident, Telles recalls the difficult position he faced. "It was like fighting in the dark. You can't really see what you're fighting—people accusing you of doing things that aren't right. It just wasn't very pleasant." He believes that much of the problem was that the public just did not know all the facts surrounding his particular business relationship with Kemp.[34]

Maury Kemp was not so fortunate as Telles. Although he was not convicted of the charges based on the two sets of indictments, he nevertheless was eventually convicted on charges of conspiracy and fraud based on his issuance of false checks related to some of his business activities. He served a minor sentence in a Texas state prison.[35]

Although a crisis in Telles's career, the Kemp-related difficulties did not irreparably harm his stature, especially in his hometown. Many El Pasoans never were convinced that he was guilty of any wrongdoing or that he had knowingly been involved in Kemp's questionable activities. If anything, many believed that Telles and his reputation had been used by his employer. According to Richard Telles, Kemp had possessed a good business and personal reputation when Raymond decided to join the firm and there had been no reason for his brother to have believed that Kemp might be involved in nebulous business practices.[36] Richard acknowledges that despite his brother's innocence, the whole Kemp episode deeply wounded his older sibling. "All this really hurt Raymond," Richard observes. "It sunk into him. Raymond is extremely sensitive. All this really hurt."[37]

Telles was not convicted or found guilty of any illegality; still the Kemp crisis represented one of the few downsides to an otherwise illustrative career. Yet it would be unfair and insensitive to assess and to judge an entire career in public service to community and to country, as in Telles's case, by one episode. Raymond Telles is much more than just the Kemp affair. It is the depth and breadth of his life and career that historians and others should judge in determining his place in history. From this perspective, his stature and importance to El Paso's history and to that of the United States remains an honored one.

Many El Pasoans, both Mexican Americans and Anglo Americans, appreciated Telles's long-term contributions and accomplishments and this recognition helped to sustain Telles through the First Financial ordeal. El Pasoans expressed deep affection for this native son of the border who rose from the barrio to become mayor of their city and the most recognized El Pasoan, in a political sense, in the country. Since he had returned to El Paso in 1982, Telles was bestowed a variety of honors by his community. These included being recognized as a Centennial Leader by the El Paso Council on Aging. LULAC Council 8 named a special community leadership award in his name. The El Paso County Democratic party inducted him into its Hall of Fame. To further honor Telles, the El Paso School Board in 1994 named a new vocational school located just a few blocks away from the old Telles home on South St. Vrain Street after him. Of this last honor, his younger daughter, Patricia, poignantly wrote to the school board:

> I congratulate the Board of Education of the city of El Paso on naming this building after a man who not only recognizes and promotes the importance of a good education, but who sincerely believes in the right to be educated. How do I know all this about Raymond Telles, Jr.? I know because he is my father and life-long teacher who instilled in me the value of learning.
>
> Raymond Telles has been a wonderful father. Through him I learned about commitment, patience, integrity, and self-respect. He taught me that a solid foundation based on principles and knowledge can lead to a successful future. "An education is the best gift you can give yourself." He often said, "No one can take away what you gained through your studies. An education is a tool that opens doors and helps build dreams. You must take advantage of this opportunity."
>
> He empowered my sister Cynthia and me with many educational opportunities. Together we have invested over 40 years in scholastic pursuits. I guess we learned our lesson well. I hope the future students of Raymond Telles Academy will feel my father's spirit and enthusiasm for learning which have been so important and rewarding in my life.
>
> Thank you Daddy for sharing your belief and dreams and thank you Mommy for supporting Cynthia and me throughout our educational endeavors. I love you,
>
> Patricia[38]

Of these honors, Telles remarked to a reporter: "Being told every once in a while that I've done a fair job at something means a lot to me."[39]

Telles was likewise bolstered by the support of his family. This included his wife, Delfina, and his two daughters, Cynthia and Patricia, both of whom have gone on from being little girls at the time of the historic election of their father as mayor of El Paso to their own professional careers and with their own families. Cynthia, a graduate of Smith College, completed a Ph.D. in clinical psychology from Boston University. She is a professor in the Department of Psychiatry and the Biobehavioral Institute of the University of California at Los Angeles (UCLA) School of Medicine. Cynthia named her son Raymond in honor of her father. Patricia graduated from Duke University and received a Ph.D. in education and counseling psychology from Boston University. She is a professor of counseling and psychological education at Florida International University in Miami.[40]

Then, of course, there were Telles's two brothers, José and Richard, who with their own extended families stood by the patriarch of the Telles clan. Raymond Telles also appreciated the continuity within the family of civic responsibility as exhibited by many of the younger generation, including his nephew, Raymond Telles III, Richard's son. He was elected to the city council in 1993 and ran for mayor in 1997 in an unsuccessful attempt to follow in his uncle's footsteps on the fortieth anniversary of the historic 1957 election. Despite the young Telles's loss, two other Mexican Americans rounded out the slate of candidates for the mayoral position, ensuring the election of one of them, Carlos Ramírez, as only the third mayor of Mexican American extraction in El Paso's history. Yet with no Anglo candidates for mayor for the first time in El Paso's political history and with a still growing Hispanic population in the border city, it is possible that the future will see continued Mexican American control of the city's highest office.

This Mexican American political ascendance in El Paso is due to the legacy of Raymond Telles and of his courageous colleagues in the 1957 campaign.

CHAPTER SEVEN

Telles's Political Legacy

The fruits of Raymond Telles's political legacy lie less in his mayoral administration and in his subsequent diplomatic and public career than in his election as mayor of El Paso in 1957. It symbolized the struggles by Mexican Americans in this border city and elsewhere for full recognition as American citizens. Mexican American leaders in El Paso viewed electoral success as the most important public vehicle for achieving political respectability and status with Anglos. Hence, Telles's election was a major victory for them. He became the first mayor of Mexican American descent in a significant southwestern city years before others such as Henry Cisneros in San Antonio and Federico Peña in Denver. Unlike those two, Telles had no Mexican American precursors as big city mayors nor access to a political culture, developed by the 1970s, that fostered open electoral alliances between Mexican Americans and Anglos. Indeed, his capable leadership as mayor and his ability to transcend ethnic politics while in office helped create the model that both Cisneros and Peña sought to emulate.

*Ambassador Raymond
L. Telles, 1990.
Courtesy* El Paso Times

Moreover, Telles's election revealed the ability of Mexican Americans to successfully organize behind one of their own candidates. Led by the likes of Richard Telles, they came to understand local politics and how to maneuver and overcome the obstacles to their electoral success. They did not overthrow the established political culture of El Paso but used it against itself through the application of political talent, skillful organization, and much hard work and dedication to a cause. The 1957 election in turn forced the Anglo establishment—the Kingmakers—to respect the political influence that Mexican Americans could wield if they chose to do so. The Anglo elite did not lose either of its dominant economic and political positions as a result of this election. However, 1957 made the Kingmakers accept a "culture of accommodation" in which Mexican Americans exercised a greater role in the governing of the city. Telles's political success also encouraged other Mexican Americans to run for substantive electoral offices. Some succeeded and some failed, but they would increase their political representation in the city council, in county government, and as representatives from El Paso to the state house in Austin, even though they would not recapture the mayor's office until 1977.

Beyond politics, Telles's election as mayor and his visible presence as head of a city with half of its population being of Mexican descent served to inspire a younger generation of Mexican Americans. As a role model, he socialized this generation to believe that they also could personally succeed in whatever endeavor they chose and that they did not have to settle for second-best. On a personal note, as I came of age in El Paso in the late 1950s and early 1960s I recall the pride I felt that a person of Mexican background—Raymond Telles—was mayor of my hometown and was later an ambassador. I dreamt of one day becoming an ambassador. I did not; nevertheless, the image of Telles spurred me on to achieve success in my own field of endeavor.

The Telles legacy further added to the Mexican American culture of struggle. Finally, his election marked the coming of political age of post–World War II Mexican Americans—what I and others have called the Mexican American Generation—throughout the Southwest.[1] Having fought and sacrificed for the survival of American democracy, they believed they could capably administer the civic and political life of their home communities.

Yet the Telles legacy is not without its shortcomings. His departure in 1961, for example, left an immense political vacuum for Mexican Americans in El Paso. They had not enough time to develop a cadre of political leaders that could step into the void. More important, activists such as Richard Telles failed to adapt their political strategies to changes in the Mexican American community. Richard, especially in his own subsequent political career as county commissioner and later as school board member, continued to apply his organizing talents to the south side. Yet in so doing, he neglected to expand his leadership and organization to the growing Mexican American neighborhoods in what had earlier been predominantly Anglo sections of the city. More acculturated than the south-siders, these Mexican Americans were more

*Reunion of the People's Ticket on the fortieth anniversary
of the historic 1957 election, 2 April 1997
(Left to right): Ralph Seitsinger, Ted Bender, Jack White,
Raymond Telles, Ernest Craigo.*
Courtesy El Paso Times

educated and in many cases had access to better jobs including middle-class professions. Consequently, no effective and comprehensive political mechanism survived after Mayor Telles's departure that could possibly duplicate the 1957 success.

Furthermore, his election and his administration did not and could not fundamentally alter the class position of most Mexican Americans as a source of cheap labor, whether blue or white collar. The Telles administration, along with addressing the needs of the city's economy, fostered better jobs for Mexican Americans but did not advance their control and power over economic resources based on commerce, banking, transportation, and industry. It would take more than electoral politics to do this. Mexican Americans through the Telles campaign pursued electoral politics in the hope of achieving status but failed to develop a consciousness and strategy to transform the most urgent reality along the border: the system of a secondary cheap labor market that resulted in disparities of wealth between themselves and Anglos and which denied Mexican Americans economic power. Telles raised the aspirations and expectations of his fellows but satisfied only the political and not the material ones. Frustration with persistent uneven economic development plus continued political and cultural discrimination yielded in the 1960s to more radical challenges by younger Chicanos, especially those from the hard-core barrios.

The limits as well as the successes of the Telles legacy raise key issues and lessons for Mexican American politics. First, his election and the level of Mexican American organization behind it belie those who have suggested that Mexican Americans are too divided and individualistic to succeed in electoral politics. The later victories of Cisneros and Peña are additional chapters to what is in fact a longer history of Mexican American political campaigns. At the same time, the Telles legacy also teaches that electoral politics by itself cannot change fundamental adverse conditions affecting Mexican Americans. Electoral politics has to go beyond the "politics of status" and instead should be one facet of a multidimensional struggle to achieve not only political power, but economic and social parity as well. Electing a Mexican American mayor, councilman, state representative, or congressman can only be the beginning of such a struggle and not its termination. Finally, the limits of the Telles experiment attest to the need to combine electoral politics with broad-based community organization aimed at achieving political, economic, and social reforms for Mexican Americans. The effectiveness of groups such as COPS (Community Organized for Public Service) in San Antonio, UNO (United Neighborhoods Organization) in Los Angeles, and EPISO (El Paso Interreligious Sponsoring Organization) in El Paso signal the commencement of this type of organization.[2] Only through grassroots community mobilization in conjunction with political campaigns can Mexican Americans begin to alter power relations in the Southwest and elsewhere and achieve the full measure of democracy for themselves and their children. The Telles legacy by itself did not fulfill this dream, but it represents, as historian Vincent Harding attributes to early black struggles in the United States, one current of the "river that moves toward a freedom that liberates the whole person and humanizes the entire society."[3]

N O T E S

INTRODUCTION: THE POLITICS OF STATUS

1. Oscar J. Martínez, *The Chicanos of El Paso: An Assessment of Progress* (El Paso: Texas Western Press, 1980), 6.
2. See Mario T. García, *Desert Immigrants: The Mexicans of El Paso, 1880–1920* (New Haven: Yale University Press, 1981). Also see Mario Barrera, *Race and Class in the Southwest: A Theory of Racial Inequality* (Notre Dame: University of Notre Dame Press, 1979); Albert Camarillo, *Chicanos in a Changing Society: From Mexican Pueblos to American Barrios in Santa Barbara and Southern California, 1848–1930* (Cambridge: Harvard University Press, 1979); Lawrence Cardoso, *Mexican Emigration to the United States, 1897–1931* (Tucson: University of Arizona Press, 1980); Arnoldo De León, *The Tejano Community, 1836–1900* (Albuquerque: University of New Mexico Press, 1982); Arnoldo De León, *They Call Them Greasers: Anglo Attitudes Toward Mexicans in Texas 1821–1900* (Austin: University of Texas Press, 1983); Richard Griswold del Castillo, *The Los Angeles Barrio, 1850–1890—A Social History* (Berkeley: University of California Press, 1979); Mark Reisler, *By the Sweat of Their Brow: Mexican Immigrant Labor in the United States* (Westport, Conn.: Greenwood Press, 1976); and Robert J. Rosenbaum, *Mexicano Resistance in the Southwest: The Sacred Right of Self-Preservation* (Austin: University of Texas Press, 1981).
3. See "Border Politics" in García, *Desert Immigrants*, 155–71.
4. See Carl Allsup, *The American G.I. Forum: Origins and Evolution* (Austin: Mexican American Center, 1982.); Luis Arroyo, "Chicano Participation in Organized Labor: The CIO in Los Angeles,

167

1938–1950: An Extended Research Note." *Aztlán* 6 (Summer 1975): 277–303; Albert Camarillo, "Research Note on Chicano Community Leaders: The G.I. Generation." *Aztlán* 2 (Fall 1971): 145–50; Richard A. García, "The Mexican American Mind: A Product of the 1930s." In Mario T. García and Francisco Lomelí, eds., *History, Culture and Society: Chicano Studies in the 1980s* (Tempe: Bilingual Press, 1983), 67–94; Edward Garza, "L.U.L.A.C." (Unpublished M.A. thesis, Southwest Texas State Teachers College, 1951); Ralph Guzmán, *The Political Socialization of the Mexican American People* (New York: Arno Press, 1976); Beatrice Griffith, *American Me* (Boston: Houghton Mifflin, 1946); Raul Marin, *Among the Valiant: Mexican Americans in World War II and Korea* (Los Angeles: Borden Publishing Co., 1963); Alonso S. Perales, *Are We Good Neighbors* (San Antonio: Artes Gráficas, 1948); Guadalupe San Miguel, "Mexican American Organizations and the Changing Politics of School Desegregation in Texas, 1945 to 1980." *Social Science Quarterly* 63 (December 1982): 701–15; Francis Jerome Woods, *Mexican Ethnic Leadership in San Antonio, Texas* (Washington, D.C.: Catholic University Press, 1949); Mario T. García, *Mexican Americans: Leadership, Ideology and Identity, 1930–1960* (New Haven: Yale University Press, 1989); Richard A. García, *Rise of the Mexican American Middle Class: San Antonio, 1929–1941* (College Station: Texas A&M University Press, 1990); Mario T. García, *Memories of Chicano History: The Life and Narrative of Bert Corona* (Berkeley and Los Angeles: University of California Press, 1994); Benjamin Márquez, *LULAC: The Evolution of a Mexican American Political Organization* (Austin: University of Texas Press, 1993).

5. Everett Ladd, Jr., *Negro Political Leadership in the South* (Ithaca: Cornell University Press, 1966), 156.

6. Ibid.

7. See García, *Desert Immigrants,* and Oscar J. Martínez, *Border Boom Town: Ciudad Juárez Since 1848* (Austin: University of Texas Press, 1980).

8. See Martínez, *Chicanos of El Paso.*

9. Marsh and Gertrude Adams, "A Report on Politics in El Paso." (Cambridge: Joint Center for Urban Studies of Massachusetts Institute of Technology and Harvard, n.d.), I–9.

10. Martínez, *Chicanos of El Paso,* 10, 12.

11. William V. D'Antonio and William H. Form, *Influentials in Two Border Cities: A Study in Community Decision-Making* (Notre Dame: University of Notre Dame Press, 1965), 20.

12. Carey McWilliams, "The El Paso Story." *The Nation* (10 July 1948): 46.
13. Martínez, *Chicanos of El Paso*, 18–19.
14. McWilliams, "The El Paso Story." 46.

CHAPTER ONE: THE YOUNG RAYMOND TELLES

1. Interview with Raymond L. Telles, 30 September 1982 and 3 May 1996; also interview with Richard Telles, 2 May 1996.
2. Ibid.
3. Raymond L. Telles to Mario T. García, El Paso, 22 July 1997. Hereinafter referred to as Telles letter.
4. Raymond Telles interview, 3 May 1996.
5. Ibid. and interview of 30 September 1982.
6. Ibid. and Richard Telles interview, 2 May 1996; Telles letter.
7. Ibid.; Telles letter.
8. Raymond Telles interview, 30 September 1982.
9. For a discussion of education of Mexicans in El Paso, see "The Mexican Schools" in García, *Desert Immigrants*, 110–20. Also oral history transcript interview with Telles by Oscar J. Martínez, 22 October 1975, Institute of Oral History, University of Texas at El Paso, 31.
10. Telles interview, 30 September 1982.
11. Telles interview, 3 May 1996; also see García, *Memories of Chicano History* and García, *Mexican Americans*.
12. Telles interview, 30 September 1982; Richard Telles interview, 2 May 1996; Telles letter.
13. See *The Chaparral*, the Cathedral High yearbook, for 1929–1933.
14. Telles interview, 3 May 1996.
15. Ibid.; Telles interview, 30 September 1982; Telles letter.
16. Telles interview, 3 May 1996; see *The Chaparral* for 1929–1933.
17. Telles interview, 3 May 1996.
18. See *The Chaparral*, 1933.
19. Telles interview, 3 May 1996.
20. Ibid.; Telles interview, 30 September 1982.
21. Telles interview, 3 May 1996.
22. Telles interview, 30 September 1982.
23. Ibid.; Telles interview, 3 May 1996; Telles letter.
24. Telles interview, 30 September 1982.

25. Ibid.

26. Ibid.

27. Telles interview, 3 May 1996; also see clipping on Delfina Navarro from a 1942 El Paso newspaper announcing her engagement to Raymond Telles in Telles File, in *Times-Herald-Post* Library. Hereinafter listed as Telles File. Also, interview with Delfina Telles, 9 July 1997.

28. Telles interview, 3 May 1996.

29. Telles interview, 30 September 1982.

30. Ibid.

31. See Delfina Navarro clipping, no date, in Telles File.

32. Telles interviews, 30 September 1982 and 3 May 1996.

33. Telles interview, 3 May 1996.

34. Ibid.; Telles interview, 30 September 1982; Telles letter.

35. Telles interview, 3 May 1996.

36. Ibid.; Telles letter.

37. Ibid.

38. Ibid.

39. Ibid.

40. Ibid.; Telles interview, 30 September 1982; also see "Public Relations Office File, Kelly Air Force Base," on Telles in Telles File; Telles letter.

41. Telles interview, 30 September 1982.

42. Richard Telles interview, 2 May 1996.

CHAPTER TWO: COUNTY CLERK

1. Interview with Richard Telles, 23 November 1982; Telles interview, 3 May 1996; Delfina Telles interview, 9 July 1997.

2. Interview with Raymond L. Telles, 20 October 1982; Telles interview, 3 May 1996.

3. *El Paso Times*, 16 May 1948, 1 and 13; 20 June 1948, 4.

4. Interview with David Villa, 16 December 1982; for a development of the concepts of "received leadership" and "internal leadership," see John Higham's chapter on "Leadership" in Stephen Thernstrom, ed., *Dimensions of Ethnicity* (Cambridge: Harvard University Press, 1982), 69–92; interview with Gabriel Navarrete, 6 December 1982.

5. *El Paso Herald-Post*, 12 July 1948, 1; 2 July 1948, 4; 12 July 1948, 1. "He was not a clean fighter," one writer has observed of Pooley. "With Pooley it was fang and claw. In news columns and editorials, the *Herald-Post* ripped and slashed happily, angrily, vigorously, mercilessly, and sometimes viciously at the opposition." See Steele Jones, "The El Paso Herald Post: The Pooley Years." (Unpublished M.A. thesis, Texas Western College, 1968), 8.

6. *Herald-Post*, 9 July 1948, 1; 12 July 1948, 1.

7. *Times*, 10 July 1948, 1; 13 July1948, 4; 18 July 1948, 6.

8. Ibid., 13 July 1948, 4; 17 July 1948, 1.

9. *Herald-Post*, 9 July 1948, 4; Telles interview, 20 October 1982; *Herald-Post*, 14 July 1948, 1–2.

10. Telles interview, 20 October 1982.

11. *Herald-Post*, 17 July 1948, 1; 19 July 1948, 8; 22 July 1948, 1.

12. Telles interview, 20 October 1982; Telles interview, 3 May 1996; Delfina Telles interview, 10 July 1997.

13. Richard Telles interviews, 23 November 1982 and 2 May 1996; Adams, "Politics in El Paso," 1–14.

14. Ibid.; Villa interview.

15. Telles interview, 20 October 1982; Richard Telles interview, 23 November 1982.

16. Telles interview, 20 October 1982; Richard Telles interview, 23 November 1982; Navarrete interview. The ethnic issue also surfaced in the Bean-Regan race when Regan people claimed that Bean supporters were circulating lies about Regan being anti-Mexican when he was mayor of Pecos, Texas; see *Times*, 21 July 1948, 8. Also, *Times*, 30 October 1983, 1A and 20A.

17. *Herald-Post*, 23 July 1948, 1 and 6; *Times*, 23 July 1948, 4, 6, and 15. Also see *Times*, 24 July 1948, 6; *Herald-Post*, 20 July 1948, 4.

18. Richard Telles interview, 23 November 1982; Villa interview; interview with Dr. Raymond Gardea, 10 January 1983; Telles interview, 20 October 1982; *Herald-Post*, 24 July 1981, 1.

19. Telles interview, 20 October 1982; *Times*, 25 July 1948, 1.

20. *Herald-Post*, 26 July 1948, 1; Telles interview, 20 October 1982; Navarrete interview; Richard Telles interview, 2 May 1996.

21. *Times*, 26 July 1948, 7.

22. Ibid.; *Herald-Post*, 26 July 1948, 1.

23. *Times*, 26 July 1948, 1. Also, see *Newsweek*, 9 August 1948, 19.

24. Ibid.; *Herald-Post*, 26 July 1948, 4.

25. *Herald-Post*, 25 February 1949, 18; *Times*, 29 January 1952, 15; Telles interview, 20 October 1982; *Times,* 11 May 1951, 1; 7 February 1952, 1; 28 September 1952, 18. Also see copies of Telles's resume in Telles File. In 1955 Telles was promoted to lieutenant colonel in the U.S. Air Force Reserve; *Times*, 23 February 1955, 5; Telles letter.

26. Telles interview, 3 May 1996.

27. *Times*, 7 April 1953, 16; 29 March 1955, 7-B; 21 August 1955, 3-D.

28. Telles interview, 20 October 1982.

29. Editor Pooley of the *Herald-Post* was liberal in supporting a more democratic electoral process in El Paso that would include Mexican Americans, but at the same time considered himself an economic conservative who endorsed Dwight Eisenhower for president in the 1950s. See Jones, "The Pooley Years."

30. *Herald-Post*, 28 February 1949, 4 and 9; see news accounts in both the *Times* and the *Herald-Post* for February 1951; *Herald-Post*, 20 February 1953, 16, and 23 February 1953, 1.

31. *Herald-Post*, 19 July 1954, 1; 26 July 1954, 1 and 16.

32. *Herald-Post*, 28 February 1955, 1.

33. *Herald-Post*, 18 February 1955, 1; 22 February 1955, 1; 25 February 1955, 1.

34. *Times*, 26 February 1955, 1; 1 March 1955; 4 March 1955, 1.

35. *Herald-Post*, 7 March 1955, 5 and 18.

36. *Herald-Post*, 25 February 1949, 25; 20 July 1950, 1 and 8; 19 July 1954, 1; 19 February 1951, 1 and 12; 22 February 1951, 1 and 10; 26 February 1951, 1–2; 18 February 1955, 1; 7 March 1955, 5; 23 July 1952, 16; 28 July 1952, 7.

37. *Herald-Post*, 22 February 1951, 1.

38. *Times*, 4 March 1951, 1; interview with Luciano Santoscoy, 8 November 1982.

39. *Herald-Post*, 1 March 1955, 18.

CHAPTER THREE: THE 1957 ELECTION

1. *Times*, 9 January 1995, 1; interview with Raymond L Telles, 16 November 1982; interview with Francisco "Kiko" Hernández, 9 November 1982; interview with Alfredo "Lelo" Jacques, 18 November 1982. A more condensed version of Chapters Three and Four can be found in García, *Mexican Americans*, 113–41.

2. Telles interview, 16 November 1982; Telles letter.
3. Interview with Albert Armendáriz, 26 October 1982.
4. Ibid.
5. Telles letter.
6. *Times*, 6 January 1957, 6-A.
7. *Times*, 12 January 1957, 1; 13 January 1957, 6-A; 14 January 1957, 4; D'Antonio and Form, *Influentials in Two Border Cities*, 138.
8. Richard Telles interview, 2 May 1996.
9. Telles interview, 16 November 1982.
10. Ibid.; interview with Ted Bender, 13 December 1982; interview with Ralph Seitsinger, 8 December 1982; *Herald-Post,* 6 and 25 February 1957, 1; Telles letter.
11. *Herald-Post*, 22 January 1957, 1 and 4; also *Times*, 23 January 1957, 1.
12. Telles letter.
13. Telles interview, 16 November 1982; *Times*, 6 February 1957, 1; interview with Ray Marantz, 25 October 1982.
14. *Herald-Post*, 23 January 1957, 2; Armendáriz interview; Hernández interview; see Telles flyers in Natalie Gross Collection, 1848-1975, Box 825, Southwest Collection, El Paso Public Library; interview with Conrad Ramírez, 2 November 1982; *Herald-Post*, 16 March 1957, 1; Richard Telles interview; *El Continental*, 24 January 1957, 1 and 6.
15. Armendáriz interview; Jacques interview; *Times*, 28 February 1957, 1; *Herald-Post*, 26 February 1957, 1 and 2; *Times*, 23 February 1957, 1; Telles letter. The *Herald-Post* noted that the total number of county registered voters had set a record at 44,437. It stressed, however, that another 100,000 voters might have registered if not for the poll tax. "There should be no poll tax, of course," it suggested. "It is a device to restrict the number of voters. . . . Citizens should not have to pay to exercise their right to choose their officials," *Herald-Post*, 1 February 1957, 22 and 5 February 1957, 18.
16. *Times*, 23 February 1957, 1.
17. *Herald-Post*, 8 and 14 February 1957; and Marantz interview.
18. *Herald-Post*, 8 and 21 February 1957.
19. *Ibid.* and 13 February 1957
20. *Herald-Post*, 8, 21 and 26 February 1957.
21. Telles interview, 16 November 1982.
22. Ibid.; Armendáriz interview.
23. Telles interview, 16 November 1982.

24. Peter K. Eisinger, *The Politics of Displacement: Racial and Ethnic Transition in Three American Cities* (New York: Academic Press, 1980), 82; *Times*, 9 and 26 February 1957.

25. *Times*, 3, 16, 26, and 27 February 1957.

26. *Times*, 12, 13, 14, 16, 21, and 27 February 1957.

27. *Times*, 14, 20, 23, 24, and 25 February 1957.

28. Eisinger, *Politics of Displacement*, 83.

29. *Times*, 23 February 1957, 1; *Herald-Post*, 15 and 22 February 1957. Former mayor Dan Ponder stated in his endorsement of Rogers: "I think it would be a disgrace for the people of El Paso to turn out such a true, tested and proven public servant as Tom Rogers in favor of an opportunist." *Times*, 1 March 1957, 1.

30. *Times*, 15, 16, 22 and 24 February 1957.

31. *Times*, 16, 19, 21, and 22 February 1957.

32. *Times*, 27 February 1957, 1; Telles interview, 16 November 1982; Santoscoy interview.

33. *Time*, 18 March 1957, 74.

34. *Herald-Post*, 24 January 1957, 12.

35. *Herald-Post*, 18, 20, 21, 25 and 27 February 1957.

36. *Herald-Post*, 19, 26 and 28 January 1957.

37. *Herald-Post*, 7, 8, 9, 25 and 30 January 1957.

38. *Herald-Post*, 22 and 23 February 1957. Fernández was convicted and fined for disturbing the peace; see *Herald-Post*, 2 March 1957, 1; also 25, 26, and 27 February 1957.

39. *Herald-Post*, 10 January 1957, 14; 21 February 1957, 1.

40. *Herald-Post,* 22, 23, 24, 26, and 27 February 1957.

41. *Herald-Post*, 25 and 26 February 1957.

42. *Herald-Post*, 31 January 1957, 18; 14, 18, and 28 February 1957.

43. William J. Hooten, *Fifty Two Years a Newsman* (El Paso: Texas Western Press, 1974), 146; *Times,* 24 February 1957, 1.

44. *Times*, 23 January 1957, 4; 8 and 9 February 1957.

45. *Times*, 24 January 1957, 4; 17, 20, 22, 24 and 25 February 1957.

46. *Times*, 1 February 1957, 1.

47. *Times*, 10, 13, 17, 23, and 28 February 1957.

48. *Times*, 25 and 28 February 1957, 1 and 2; 1 March 1957, 1.

49. *Times*, 1 March 1957, 6.

50. *El Continental*, 12 February 1957, 1; Armendáriz interview; Bender interview; Telles interview, 16 November 1982.

51. Telles interview, 16 November 1982.

52. *Times*, 20 February 1957, 4.
53. See Cleofas Calleros to W. J. Hooten, Tom E. Rogers, and Judson Williams, 23 February 1957, in Cleofas Calleros Collection, Letterbook, vol. 15, Southwest Collection, El Paso Public Library.
54. Telles interview, 16 November 1982; *Times*, 3 March 1957, 3-B; Richard Telles interview, 23 November 1982.

CHAPTER FOUR: RICHARD TELLES AND BARRIO POLITICS

1. Bender interview; Jacques interview; Richard Telles interviews, 23 November 1982 and 2 May 1996.
2. Richard Telles interviews, 23 November 1982 and 2 May 1996; Navarrete interview; Seitsinger interview.
3. Richard Telles interviews, 23 November 1982 and 2 May 1996; Hernández interview.
4. Richard Telles interviews, 23 November 1982 and 2 May 1996; Villa interview; Navarrete interview.
5. Richard Telles interview, 23 November 1982; Delfina Telles interview, 10 July 1997.
6. Ibid.; Villa interview; Hernández interview.
7. Richard Telles interview, 23 November 1982; Marantz interview; Bender interview; Hernández interview, 23 November 1982.
8. Richard Telles interview, 23 November 1982.
9. Villa interview; Armendáriz interview; Richard Telles interview, 23 November 1982.
10. Armendáriz interview.
11. Marantz interview; *Herald-Post*, 2 March 1957, 1; Telles interview, 16 November 1982. Telles at the time lived in central El Paso, at 1160 North Virginia Street.
12. Telles interview, 16 November 1982; *Times*, 3 March 1957, II-A. Eighty percent of registered voters went to the polls; Navarrete interview. Fermín Dorado, who later worked for the El Paso City Planning Department, recalls that on election eve he was at the Ascarate Drive-In Theatre in the Lower Valley. The movie was interrupted for an announcement of Telles's victory. The people honked their horns and shouted in elation at the news; interview, 15 December 1982.
13. As cited in Hooten, *Fifty-Two Years*, 149.
14. *Herald-Post*, 4 March 1957, 6; Seitsinger interview; Armendáriz interview.

15. *Herald-Post*, 4 March 1957, 1 and 6; *Times*, 3 March 1957, 1.

16. *Herald-Post*, 4 March 1957, 1, 6, and 18; *Times*, 4 March 1957, 1.

17. *Times*, 3 March 1957, 6-A; 4 March 1957, 4.

18. *Times*, 8 March 1957, 1; Telles interview, 16 November 1982; *Times*, 13, 14 and 26 March 1957.

19. *Herald-Post*, 11, 12 and 13 March 1957.

20. *Herald-Post*, 13 March 1957, 2. Voting machines had to remain sealed by law for 10 days after an election; *El Continental*, 18 March 1957, 1.

21. *Times*, 6 April 1957, 1; Telles interview, 16 November 1982; *Herald-Post*, 6 April 1957, 4.

22. *Times*, 7 April 1957, 1 and 4; 8 April 1957, 8.

23. *Times*, 8 April 1957, 1; also see letter to the editor in *Times*, 9 April 1957, 4.

24. *Times*, 8 and 9 April 1957.

25. Telles interview, 16 November 1982; *Herald-Post*, 8 April 1957, 1.

26. *Herald-Post*, 8 April 1957, 1.

27. *El Continental*, 8 April 1957, 1; *Herald-Post*, 8 April 1957, 18.

28. Richard Telles interview, 23 November 1982; *El Continental*, 3 April 1957, 1; *Times*, 9 April 1957, 1.

29. *Times*, 9 April 1951, 1; *Herald-Post*, 9 and 10 April 1957; *El Continental*, 10 April 1957, 1 and 6.

30. *Times,* 10 and 11 April 1957; *Herald-Post*, 10 April 1957, 18.

31. *El Continental*, 11 April 1957, 1.

CHAPTER FIVE: MAYOR TELLES

1. Interview with Ken Flynn, 16 November 1982; Richard Telles interview, 23 November 1982.

2. Eisinger, *Politics of Displacement*, xvii, xviii, 149, 152; also see Charles H. Levine, *Racial Conflict and the American Mayor* (Lexington, Mass: Lexington Books, 1974).

3. *Herald-Post*, March 11, 1958, 14; also see, *Times*, 30 October 1983, 1A and 20A.

4. Telles appointed approximately forty-two Mexican Americans to various city commissions; see City Council Minutes in the City Clerk's Office, El Paso City Hall; interview with Raymond L. Telles, 14 December 1982.

5. City Council, Minutes, 25 July 1957, 490 and 14 April 1960, 149; Armendáriz interview. For a count of Mexican Americans appointed to the police and fire departments see City Council, Minutes.

6. Telles letter.

7. *Herald-Post*, 30 September 1957, 1; 5 November 1958, 1 and 5; *Times*, 3 March 1959, 4.

8. D'Antonio and Form, *Influentials in Two Border Cities,* 19; *Herald-Post*, 27 March 1959, 1; and 9 January 1960, 1; Telles interview, 14 December 1982.

9. *Herald-Post*, 6, 7, 8, 10, 15, 17 and 18 March 1961; also, City Council Minutes, 14 March 1961, 476–78.

10. See various copies of Telles's resume in Telles File.

11. *Herald-Post*, 30 September 1957, 1; 28 April 1959, 15.

12. Santoscoy interview.

13. *Herald-Post*, 30 September 1957, 1; D'Antonio and Form, *Influentials in Two Border Cities*, 146.

14. Interview with Joe Herrera, 10 January 1983.

15. Eisinger, *Politics of Displacement*, 153 and 194.

16. *Times*, 4 February 1959, 3.

17. *Times*, 10 January 1959, 4. Hooten in his autobiography wrote: "Raymond Telles served two terms as mayor of El Paso. He had what I would call a 'warm' administration, constantly endeavoring to make friends with the people. He and I never were unfriendly, and in later years we became very good friends." Hooten, *Fifty-Two Years*, 149; also see *Herald-Post*, 7 April 1959, 16.

18. Telles interview, 14 December 1982. For the Democratic primary issue, see the *Times* and the *Herald-Post* during the early part of 1959; also see D'Antonio and Form, *Influentials in Two Border Cities*, 142–44; and phone interview with Raymond Telles, 26 February 1997. Although Mexican Americans have had difficulty gaining the mayor's office, in 1997 they represented a majority on the city council. Much more important to Mexican American electoral success in city elections has been the shift from citywide to district elections for council positions.

19. *Herald-Post*, 1 December 1960, 1–2; Telles interview, 3 May 1992.

20. *Herald-Post*, 3 January 1961, 1–2; *Times*, 15 February 1961, 1; and 4 January 1961, 4.

21. *Herald-Post*, 4 February 1961, 1. In the *Times*, Hooten wrote of the Telles-Bean relationship: "It has been no secret that El Paso's mayor and County Judge have been feuding for some time. Therefore, it was a surprise to read where the County Judge was 'showering' Washington with telegrams in an effort to get the mayor a federal appointment. Some wag observed that it looked as though Bean was trying to get Telles out of town." *Times*, 5 and 6 February 1961; Richard Telles interview, 2 May 1996.

22. *Times*, 4 February 1961, 1 and 14.

23. Telles interview, 3 May 1996; also see *Herald-Post*, 9 and 11 February 1961; *Times*, 10 February 1961, 4.

24. Armendáriz interview; Jacques interview; Richard Telles interview, 2 May 1996; Delfina Telles interview, 10 July 1997.

25. Richard Telles interview, 23 November 1982; Navarrete interview; Telles interview, 3 May 1996.

26. *Herald-Post*, 17 February 1961; *Times*, 17 February 1961; the *New York Times*, 16 February 1961, 5.

27. *Times*, 5 March 1961, 6-A; 18 February 1961, 4; Hernández interview; Jacques interview.

28. *Herald-Post*, 16, 17, and 23 February 1961; 3 March 1961, 1; *Times*, 19 February 1961, 6-A.

29. *Herald-Post*, 3, 24 and 27 March 1961.

30. *Herald-Post*, 3 and 8 April 1961; Adams, "Politics in El Paso," ii–34.

31. *Times*, 25 March 1961, 1 and 5.

32. *El Continental*, 30 March 1961, 3; 10 April 1961, 3; *Herald-Post*, 12, 13 and 14 April 1961.

33. *Herald-Post*, 17 April 1961, 1; *Times*, 19 April 1961, 3; Telles interview, 14 December 1982.

CHAPTER SIX: MR. AMBASSADOR

1. For Telles's accounts of his diplomatic experience, see Telles interview, 3 May 1996; also see the *New York Times* coverage of Kennedy's visit to Costa Rica especially 16, 18, 19, 20, 21, and 22 March 1963; also see Delfina Telles interview, 10 July 1997, and Telles letter.

2. See *Times*, 15 December 1963, 1 and 8A; 20 February 1964, 1; 29 December 1965, 1-B; 3 November 1966, 1; 4 January 1967, 1; 20, 22, and 23 February 1967; 28 March 1968, 8-A; 17 May 1969, 1; and interview with Telles, 13 January 1983.

3. Telles interview, 13 January 1983.

4. *Herald-Post*, 23 April 1970, D-1; 4 and 12 March 1970.

5. *Herald-Post*, 17 April 1970, 1 and 7; 4 February 1970, 2; 26 January 1970, 2.

6. *Herald-Post*, 20 March 1970, B-2; 9 April 1970, C-3; 1 May 1970, B-1; 9 and 28 April 1970.

7. Hernández interview; also see clipping from *Times*, 31 March 1970 in Telles File.

8. Navarrete interview; Hernández interview; Telles interview, 13 January 1983.

9. *Herald-Post*, 24 April 1970, B-2.

10. Telles interview, 13 January 1983.

11. *Herald-Post*, 17, 25 and 27 April 1970; 5 March 1970, 3.

12. Richard Telles interview, 23 November 1982; Santoscoy interview; *Times*, 27 March 1970, B-2; 27, 29, and 30 April 1970; 1 May 1970, 12; also clippings *Times*, 31 March 1970 in Telles File.

13. *Herald-Post*, 4 May 1970, 1, 4 and B-2; *Times*, 3 May 1970, 12-A; Telles interview, 13 January 1983.

14. Raymond Telles interview, 10 July 1997.

15. *Times*, 28 September 1971, 1-C; 4 April 1982, 3-G; and Telles interviews, 13 January 1983, and 3 May 1996; also see Richard Telles interview, 2 May 1996.

16. See *Times*, 4 April 1982 in Telles File.

17. Raymond Telles interview, 9 July 1997.

18. See *Herald-Post*, 8 April 1981 in Telles File.

19. See *Times*, 7 January 1988; 25 February 1983; 7 March 1993, 9B in Telles File.

20. *Times*, 7 March 1993, 9B.

21. See Brian W. Shaughnessy to Telles, Wash., D.C., 7 April 1976 in possession of Telles.

22. See *Times*, 4 November 1976, 2-B; 20 January 1977, 1 and 15-A; 30 October 1983, 20-A; Telles interview, 10 July 1997.

23. See various clippings in Telles File especially *Herald-Post*, 5 November 1976 and *Times*, 20 January 1977.

24. Telles interview, 9 July 1997.

25. See newspaper clippings on the First Financial scandal in Telles File; Telles interview, 9 July 1997.

26. See *Times*, 28 June and 18 September 1988 in Telles File.

27. See *Times*, 4 and 19 January 1989; 31 August 1989; 17 October 1989 in Telles File; see documents related to Kemp's operations in possession of Telles; Telles interview, 9 July 1997.

28. *Times*, 18 September 1988, 6A; Telles interview, 9 July 1997.

29. See Kemp news release, 13 October 1988 in possession of Telles.

30. Telles interview, 9 July 1997; Telles letter.

31. *Times*, 1 December 1990; 6 June 1991; 7 June 1991; and copies of the indictments in Telles File; Telles interview, 9 July 1997.

32. See pertinent documents in possession of Telles and Telles interview, 9 July 1997; also see *Times*, 16 July 1992 in Telles File.

33. *Times*, 16 July 1992 in Telles File.

34. Telles interview, 9 July 1997; also see *Times*, 16 July 1992 in Telles File.

35. Telles interview, 9 July 1997.

36. Richard Telles interview, 2 May 1996.

37. Ibid.

38. See *Herald-Post*, 30 May 1986; clipping, 16 November 1985; undated clipping all in Telles File. Also, Patricia Telles to El Paso School Board, 18 May 1994, in possession of Raymond Telles.

39. Clipping, 30 May 1986, in Telles File.

40. See *Herald-Post*, 17 January 1994 and Telles resume in Telles File.

CHAPTER SEVEN: TELLES'S POLITICAL LEGACY

1. Camarillo, "Research Note on Chicano Community Leaders."

2. See Peter Skerry, *Mexican Americans: The Ambivalent Minority* (New York: The Free Press, 1993).

3. Vincent Harding, *There is a River: The Black Struggle for Freedom in America* (New York: Vintage Books, 1983), xxiv.

BIBLIOGRAPHY

PRIMARY SOURCES

Newspapers and News Magazines
El Paso Herald-Post
El Paso Times
El Continental
New York Times
Newsweek
Time

Oral History
Albert Armendáriz, 26 October 1982.
Ted Bender, 13 December 1982.
Fermín Dorado, 15 December 1982.
Ken Flynn, 16 December 1982.
Dr. Raymond Gardea, 10 January 1983.
Francisco "Kiko" Hernández, 9 November 1982.
Joe Herrera, 10 January 1983.
Alfredo "Lelo" Jacques, 18 November 1982.
Ray Marantz, 25 October 1982.
Gabriel Navarrete, 6 December 1982.
Delfina Navarro (Telles), 9 July and 10 July 1997.
Conrad Ramírez, 2 November 1982.
Luciano Santoscoy, 8 November 1982.
Ralph Seitsinger, 8 December 1982.

181

Raymond L. Telles, 30 September 1982; 20 October 1982; 16 November 1982; 14 December 1982; 13 January 1983; 3 May 1996; 26 February 1997; 9 July 1997; 10 July 1997.

Raymond L. Telles, 22 October 1975. Interviewed by Oscar J. Martínez. Institute of Oral History, University of Texas at El Paso.

Richard Telles, 23 November 1982; 2 May 1996.

David Villa, 16 December 1982.

Archival Sources

The Chaparral, 1929–33, Cathedral High School yearbook, El Paso.

City Council Minutes, 1957–1960, City Clerk's Office, El Paso City Hall.

Cleofas Calleros Collection, Letterbook, vol. 15, Southwest Collection, El Paso Public Library.

Natalie Gross Collection, 1848–1975, Box 825, Southwest Collection, El Paso Public Library.

Raymond L. Telles File in *El Paso Times–El Paso Herald-Post* Library, El Paso.

Raymond L. Telles Private Collection, El Paso.

Correspondence

Raymond L. Telles to Mario T. García, El Paso, 22 July 1997.

SECONDARY SOURCES

Books

Allsup, Carl. *The American G.I. Forum: Origins and Evolution*. Austin: Mexican American Center, 1982.

Barrera, Mario. *Race and Class in the Southwest: A Theory of Racial Inequality*. Notre Dame: University of Notre Dame Press, 1979.

Camarillo, Albert. *Chicanos in a Changing Society: From Mexican Pueblos to American Barrios in Santa Barbara and Southern California, 1848–1930*. Cambridge: Harvard University Press, 1979.

Cardoso, Lawerence. *Mexican Emigration to the United States, 1897–1931*. Tucson: University of Arizona Press, 1980.

D'Antonio, William V. and William H. Form. *Influentials in Two Border Cities: A Study in Community Decision-Making*. Notre Dame: University of Notre Dame Press, 1965.

De León, Arnoldo. *The Tejano Community, 1836–1900.* Albuquerque: University of New Mexico Press, 1982.

De León, Arnoldo. *They Call Them Greasers: Anglo Attitudes Toward Mexicans in Texas, 1821–1900.* Austin: University of Texas Press, 1983.

Eisinger, Peter K. *The Politics of Displacement: Racial and Ethnic Transition in Three American Cities.* New York: Academic Press, 1980.

García, Mario T. *Desert Immigrants: The Mexicans of El Paso, 1880–1920.* New Haven: Yale University Press, 1981.

———. *Memories of Chicano History: The Life and Narrative of Bert Corona.* Berkeley and Los Angeles: University of California Press, 1994.

———. *Mexican Americans: Leadership, Ideology and Identity.* New Haven: Yale University Press, 1989.

García, Richard A. *Rise of the Mexican American Middle Class: San Antonio, 1929–1941.* College Station: Texas A & M Press, 1990.

Griffith, Beatrice. *American Me.* Boston: Houghton Mifflin, 1946.

Griswold del Castillo, Richard. *The Los Angeles Barrio, 1850–1890—A Social History.* Berkeley: University of California Press, 1979.

Guzmán, Ralph. *The Political Socialization of the Mexican American People.* New York: Arno Press, 1976.

Harding, Vincent. *There is a River: The Black Struggle for Freedom in America.* New York: Vintage Books, 1983.

Hooten, William J. *Fifty-Two Years A Newsman.* El Paso: Texas Western Press, 1974.

Ladd, Jr., Everett. *Negro Political Leadership in the South.* Ithaca: Cornell University Press, 1966.

Levine, Charles H. *Racial Conflict and the American Mayor.* Lexington, Mass: Lexington Books, 1974.

Marin, Raul. *Among the Valiant: Mexican Americans in World War II and Korea.* Los Angeles: Borden Publishing Co., 1963.

Márquez, Benjamin. *LULAC: The Evolution of a Mexican American Political Organization.* Austin: University of Texas Press, 1993.

Martínez, Oscar J. *Border Boom Town: Ciudad Juárez Since 1848.* Austin: University of Texas Press, 1980.

Martínez, Oscar J. *The Chicanos of El Paso: An Assessment of Progress.* El Paso: Texas Western Press, 1980.

Perales, Alonso S. *Are We Good Neighbors.* San Antonio: Artes Gráficas, 1948.

Reisler, Mark. *By the Sweat of Their Brow: Mexican Immigrant Labor in the United States.* Westport, Conn.: Greenwood Press, 1976.

Rosenbaum, Robert J. *Mexicano Resistance in the Southwest: The Sacred Right of Self-Preservation.* Austin: University of Texas Press, 1981.

Skerry, Peter. *Mexican Americans: The Ambivalent Minority.* New York: The Free Press, 1993.

Woods, Francis Jerome. *Mexican Ethnic Leadership in San Antonio, Texas.* Washington, D.C.: Catholic University Press, 1949.

Articles and Book Chapters

Arroyo, Luis. "Chicano Participation in Organized Labor: The CIO in Los Angeles, 1938–1950: An Extended Research Note." *Aztlán* 6 (Summer 1975): 277–303.

Camarillo, Albert. "Research Note on Chicano Community Leaders: The G.I. Generation." *Aztlán* 2 (Fall 1971): 145–50.

García, Richard A. "The Mexican American Mind: A Product of the 1930s." In Mario T. García and Francisco Lomeli, eds., *History, Culture, and Society: Chicano Studies in the 1980s.* Tempe: Bilingual Press, 1983, 67–94.

Higham, John. "Leadership." In Stephen Thernstrom, ed., *Dimensions of Ethnicity.* Cambridge: Harvard University Press, 1982, 69–92.

McWilliams, Carey. "The El Paso Story." *The Nation* (10 July 1948): 46.

San Miguel, Guadalupe. "Mexican American Organizations and the Changing Politics of School Desegregation in Texas, 1945 to 1980." *Social Science Quarterly* 63 (December 1982): 701–15.

UNPUBLISHED MATERIAL

Adams, Marsh and Gertrude. "A Report on Politics in El Paso." Report for Joint Center for Urban Studies of Massachusetts Institute of Technology and Harvard University, n.d.

Garza, Edward. "L.U.L.A.C." M.A. thesis, Southwest Texas State Teachers College, 1951.

Jones, Steele. "The El Paso Herald Post: The Pooley Years." M.A. thesis, Texas Western College, 1968.

INDEX

185